Instant Pot Duo Crisp Air Fryer Cookbook

1000 Days of Quick And Easy Instant Pot Duo Recipes

Copyright 2020 by World Good Foods Ltd

The recipes and information in this book are provided for educational purposes only. Everyone needs are different, and these recipes and methods reflect specifically on what has worked for the author. This book is not intended to provide medical advice or take the place of medical treatment from qualified health care professionals. All readers who are taking any form of prescription medication should consult with their physicians before making any changes to their current eating habits. Neither the publisher nor the author takes any responsibility for any possible consequences of any person reading or following the information in this book.

TABLE OF CONTENTS

INTRODUCTION	4

CHICKEN — 5

Crispy Shredded Chicken	6
Chicken Hot Wings	7
Chicken Indian Kebab	8
Chicken Chimichangas	9
Tasty Chicken Wings	10
Whole Chicken Roast	11
Stuffed Chicken	12
Coconut Curry	13
Herb Crusted Chicken Breast	14
Potato Chicken Curry	15
Chicken Marsala	16

PORK — 28

Sausage with Onions	29
Garlic Bread Pizza	30
Sausage Balls	31
Pork Chops	32
Pork Fried Rice	33
Pork Stew with Veggies	34
Pork Broccoli Stir Fry	35
Pork Cashew Nut Salad	36
Pork Steak with Cauliflower	37
Green Beans Pork Bites	38

TURKEY — 17

Fried Turkey Burgers	18
Turkey Skewers	19
Coconut Crusted Turkey Balls	20
Turkey Salad	21
Crispy Turkey Strips	22
Turkey Stew	23
Turkey Casserole	24
Left-over Turkey Quiche	25
Citrus Turkey Roast	26
Stuffed Spinach Turkey Breasts	27

BEEF — 39

Crispy Chuck Roast	40
Crispy Pot Roast	41
Ribeye Fried Steak	42
Steak Bites	43
Beef Broccoli Stir Fry	44
Minced Beef Rice	45
Beef Curry	46
Beef Meatballs	47
Beef Steak	48
Beef Carrot Stew	49
Beef Pasta	50

LAMB — 51
- Asian Fried Lamb Chops — 52
- Lamb Skewers — 53
- Rosemary Lamb Chops — 54
- Garlic Honey Lamb Chops — 55
- Bell Pepper Lamb Stir Fry — 56
- Chickpea Lamb Stew — 57
- Pepper Lamb Shank — 58
- Red Chili Lamb Leg Roast — 59

VEGETARIAN — 60
- Mac & Cheese — 61
- Soy Cauliflower — 62
- Pesto Veggie Pasta — 63
- Eggplant in tomato gravy — 64
- Stuffed Zucchini — 65
- Air Fried Plantain Chips — 66
- Stuffed Bell Pepper — 67
- Tofu Cauliflower Stir fry — 68
- Broccoli Quinoa Fry — 69
- Spinach Lentil Curry — 70
- Cauliflower Soup — 71

DESSERTS — 72
- Coated Apple Chips — 73
- Air Fryer Bred Sticks — 74
- Egg Flan — 75
- Chocolate Muffin — 76
- Rice Pudding — 77
- Mango Coconut Rice Pudding — 78
- Almond Cake — 79
- Brownie — 80
- Carrot Cake — 81

FISH & SEAFOOD — 82
- Shrimp Tacos — 83
- Zesty Fish Filets — 84
- Duo Crisp Tilapia Fry — 85
- Herb Salmon — 86
- Baked Salmon — 87
- Fish Soup — 88
- Steamed Tilapia — 89
- Butter Tossed Cod with Asparagus — 90
- Tuna Steak with Baby Potatoes — 91
- Crispy Sardine Salad — 92
- Shrimp in Tomato Sauce — 93

The Schedules — 94

INSTANT POT DUO COOKBOOK

Thank you first for getting this cookbook. Here you will be provided all the tools Instant Pot Duo Books require to get started, along with delicious recipes that are quick and easy to prepare and budget friendly. I sincerely hope that you will enjoy the recipes and guidance offered in this cookbook.

As a Thank you, I would like you to join on Facebook my FREE Books Page, where you will be messaged free books, both kindle and paperback when available.

Click on the link below and start enjoying them from today!

https://bit.ly/BooksGaloreFree

CHICKEN RECIPES

CRISPY SHREDDED CHICKEN

Prep Time: 15 min   **Servings: 6**   **Kcal: 650**

INGREDIENTS

4 cups shredded chicken	10 oz egg noodles	1 onion
1 cup chopped carrots	1 cup frozen peas	½ frozen broccoli florets
2 celery stalks	7 cups chicken broth	4 tsp garlic powder, salt and pepper
1 cup cheddar	1 can mushroom soup	½ cup sour cream

DIRECTIONS

1. Drop chicken, garlic powder, salt & pepper, broth and vegetables into the pot and mix well.
2. Stir in the noodles until well soaked and covered.
3. Seal the pressure-cooking lid and select high pressure for 5 minutes, then apply a fast release.
4. Mix in the mushroom soup can, cheese and cream.
5. Seal the frying lid and air fry at 400 F for 5 minutes.
6. Remove from pot and serve hot.

CHICKEN HOT WINGS

Prep Time: 45 min   **Servings:** 4   **Kcal:** 600

INGREDIENTS

- 16 chicken wings
- 1 cup hot sauce
- 1 tsp Worcestershire sauce
- 1 tsp garlic powder
- 2 tbsp olive oil
- 1 ½ cup chicken broth
- 2 tsp vinegar
- Salt to taste
- 2 cups chicken broth
- ½ cup butter
- 1 tsp black pepper
- Celery to decorate

DIRECTIONS

1. Drop the broth into the pot.
2. Put the wings into the air frying basket and place it into the pot.
3. Close the lid for pressure cooking and apply high pressure for 11 minutes. Then apply a quick release for the pressure.
4. In the meantime, put the butter, sauces, pepper, garlic powder and vinegar in a pan.
5. Let the pan heat the ingredients until bubbly. The set aside the contents.
6. Take out the air frying basket and discard the liquid remaining inside the instant pot.
7. Spray some oil on the wings and mix. Coat well.
8. Add salt and pepper on the wings.
9. Seal the air frying lid and apply air frying mode at 400 F, tossing and flipping the chicken every 3 minutes.
10. Serve with desired dressing and decorate with the celery.

CHICKEN INDIAN KEBAB

Prep Time: 25 min   **Servings:** 6   **Kcal:** 475

INGREDIENTS

- 1 ½ lb. chicken thighs
- 1 ½ cup mix of cubed green and red peppers
- 1 tbsp ginger
- 1 tbsp chili powder
- 2 tsp coriander powder
- 2 tbsp olive oil
- Lime wedges to garnish
- 1 tbsp garlic
- 1 tsp turmeric
- Salt to taste
- 1 cup sliced onion
- ¾ cups full fat Greek yogurt
- 2 tbsp lime juice
- 2 tsp Garam Masala

DIRECTIONS

1. Mix the marinade ingredients on a bowl and then coat the chicken well into the mixture before leaving it to rest for 5 hours.
2. Now add peppers, oil and onions to the marinated mixture.
3. Thread the ingredients into skewers.
4. Brush the crisp air fryer basket with oil. Make sure the skewers and well coated with oil before placing them in.
5. Plate the trivet in the inner pot and place basket on top of the trivet.
6. Set the lid over the pot and plug well in. Set air frying mode to 400 F for 10 minutes.
7. Once time is up, flip the skewers and cook for further 8 minutes.
8. Serve warm with desired decoration.

CHICKEN CHIMICHANGAS

Prep Time: 25 min   **Servings:** 6   **Kcal:** 550

INGREDIENTS

- 1 shredded rotisserie chicken
- ½ cup salt
- ½ cup Cheese sauce
- ½ cup sour cream
- 2 cups cooked rice
- 12 soft taco tortillas
- Shredded lettuce to taste
- ½ cup guacamole
- 1 ½ cup salsa
- 3 tsp vegetable oil
- 3 Diced tomatoes

DIRECTIONS

1. Preheat air fryer after brushing some oil to 350 F.
2. Mix in a bowl the salsa, salt and chicken well.
3. Drop evenly chicken filling in the middle of each tortilla and roll them up tight by folding the ends.
4. Drop the chimichangas in the air frying basket, top with some vegetable oil. and seal the lid.
5. Air fry for 5 minutes at 350 F.
6. After this, open the lid and flip them over. Close the lid and air fry for 5 minutes longer.
7. Top the chimichangas with cheese sauce, tomato, lettuce, guacamole and sour cream.

TASTY CHICKEN WINGS

Prep Time: 35 min **Servings:** 6 **Kcal:** 133

INGREDIENTS

- 12 chicken wings
- 1 tbsp avocado oil
- 1 cup chicken stock
- 1 tsp dried oregano
- Sea salt to taste
- 1 tsp garlic powder
- 2 tbsp soy sauce
- 1 tsp ginger powder
- Pepper to taste

DIRECTIONS

1. Add the chicken stock into the instant pot.
2. Fill the air fryer basket with the chicken wings.
3. Cover with the lid and pressure cook for around 10 minutes.
4. Release the pressure for the instant pot and drain the liquid.
5. Add the avocado oil, and toss the chicken wings.
6. Add the sea salt, pepper, garlic powder, ginger powder, oregano and soy sauce.
7. Coat well and turn the temperature to 400 degrees F.
8. Lock the air fryer's lid and air fry for about 5 minutes.
9. Toss again and air fry for another 10 minutes.
10. Toss one last time and air fry for 10 minutes. Serve with any dipping sauce of your choice.

WHOLE CHICKEN ROAST

Prep Time: 60 min   **Servings:** 4   **Kcal:** 223

INGREDIENTS

1 whole chicken	1 tsp oregano	1 lemon, sliced
Sea salt to taste	2 tsp red chili powder	2 tbsp olive oil
Pepper to taste	1 tsp garlic powder	1 cup chicken broth
2 tsp thyme	1 tsp ginger powder	

DIRECTIONS

1. In a bowl, combine the sea salt, pepper, thyme, oregano, red chili powder, garlic, ginger, olive oil and mix well.
2. Coat the chicken in the mixture finely and add the lemon slices as a stuffing.
3. Let it sit for 10 minutes. Add the chicken into the Instant pot.
4. Turn on the sauté option on and cook for 5 minutes.
5. Carefully flip the chicken over and cook for another 5 minutes.
6. Add a trivet into the instant pot and pour in the chicken broth. Add the chicken on top of the trivet.
7. Change the cooking mode to pressure cooking and select the high pressure option.
8. Cover and cook for 30 minutes. Release the pressure. Let the chicken rest for 10 minutes and then serve hot.

STUFFED CHICKEN

Prep Time: 15 min   **Servings:** 2   **Kcal:** 301

INGREDIENTS

2 chicken breasts
½ tsp paprika
2 mozzarella cheese slices
4 tbsp feta cheese
1 cup water
Sea salt and pepper to taste
4 asparagus
1 tsp olive oil

DIRECTIONS

1. Trim the asparagus and set aside for now. Remove the bones from the chicken breasts.
2. Combine the feta cheese, paprika together and add onto the chicken breasts.
3. Add the mozzarella cheese slices and 2 asparagus into each chicken breast and roll them tightly and seal using a kitchen thread.
4. Sprinkle some sea salt and pepper on top. Choose the sauté option in your instant pot and add the olive oil.
5. Add the chicken breasts and cook until the outer layer becomes crispy.
6. Take out the chicken and place a trivet into the instant pot.
7. Pour in your water and add the chicken pieces on top of the trivet.
8. Cover and cook on high pressure mode for 8 minutes.
9. Release the pressure and let it rest for 10 minutes and then cut into thick slices.
10. Serve.

COCONUT CHICKEN CURRY

Prep Time: 25 min   **Servings:** 4   **Kcal:** 469

INGREDIENTS

4 chicken thighs
2 white onion, diced
1 tsp ginger paste
1 tsp garlic paste

2 cup coconut milk
2 bay leaves
1 cinnamon stick
Salt and pepper to taste

1 tsp butter
½ tsp paprika
½ tsp cumin
1 tsp coriander powder

DIRECTIONS

1. Remove the skin and bones of the chicken thighs and cut into medium cubes.
2. In your instant pot, add the butter, chicken cubes, white onion, ginger paste, garlic paste, bay leaves, cinnamon stick, salt, pepper, paprika, cumin, coriander powder and coconut milk.
3. Cover with the lid. Choose high pressure cooking and set the timer to 15 minutes.
4. After 15 minutes, release the pressure and wait for 10 minutes. Serve.

HERB CRUSTED CHICKEN BREASTS

Prep Time: 30 min   **Servings:** 2   **Kcal:** 213

INGREDIENTS

- 2 chicken breasts
- 1 tsp chives, minced
- 1 tsp thyme, minced
- 1 tsp rosemary, minced
- 2 tbsp breadcrumbs
- 2 tsp parmesan cheese
- Salt and pepper to taste
- 1 tbsp olive oil
- ½ tsp paprika
- 1 cup chicken stock

DIRECTIONS

1. Remove the skin and bone from the chicken breasts.
2. In a bowl, combine the chives, thyme, rosemary, breadcrumbs, parmesan cheese, salt, pepper, and paprika.
3. Mix well and coat the chicken in it. Let it sit for 10 minutes. Add the olive oil into the instant pot.
4. Add the chicken and sauté for 3 minutes on each side.
5. Take out the chicken and place a trivet into the instant pot.
6. Pour in your chicken stock and add the chicken pieces on top of the trivet.
7. Cover and cook on high pressure mode for 8 minutes.
8. Release the pressure and then wait for 10 minutes before serving.

POTATO CHICKEN CURRY

Prep Time: 50 min   **Servings:** 4   **Kcal:** 367

INGREDIENTS

1 whole chicken	2 onion, chopped	1 tbsp oil
½ cup yogurt	4 garlic cloves, minced	2 tsp cumin & salt
1 cup potato, halved	1 tsp ginger, minced	1 tsp coriander
2 cup chicken stock	1 tsp turmeric	2 tsp paprika & pepper

DIRECTIONS

1. Cut the chicken into medium pieces. Keep the bones and skin.
2. Marinate the chicken using yogurt, turmeric, salt, pepper, cumin, coriander and paprika.
3. Let it sit for 20 minutes. Put the sauté option on in your instant pot.
4. Add the oil and sauté the garlic, ginger and onion for 2 minutes.
5. Add the chicken mix, potatoes and chicken stock into the instant pot.
6. Turn the high-pressure cooking option. Cover and cook for 15 minutes.
7. Release the pressure and then wait for 10 minutes. Serve hot.

CHICKEN MARSALA

Prep Time: 25 min   **Servings:** 2   **Kcal:** 416

INGREDIENTS

2 chicken breasts

Salt and pepper to taste

1 tbsp olive oil

2 tbsp flour

2 tbsp butter

4 garlic cloves, minced

1 cup mushroom

½ cup marsala wine

½ cup chicken stock

1 tbsp corn flour

2 tbsp water

DIRECTIONS

1. Cut the chicken breasts into lengthwise cutlets.
2. Sprinkle some salt, pepper onto the chicken pieces.
3. Choose the sauté option in your instant pot and melt half the butter.
4. Sauté the chicken until it becomes brown. Turn off the sauté option.
5. Pour in the chicken stock, marsala wine, garlic, mushrooms, olive oil, and cover with lid.
6. Choose the high-pressure cooking option and cook for 6 minutes.
7. Release the pressure and take the chicken out.
8. In a bowl, combine the corn flour, water, flour, and mix well.
9. Add this mixture and the remaining butter to the instant pot and stir well.
10. Cover and simmer for 5 minutes. Pour the sauce on top of the chicken and serve hot.

TURKEY RECIPES

FRIED TURKEY BURGERS

Prep Time: 25 min   **Servings:** 6   **Kcal:** 513

INGREDIENTS

2 small eggs

1/3 cup breadcrumbs

1/3 cup milk

1 tsp pepper

2 tsp garlic powder

1 tsp onion powder

1 tsp poultry seasoning

1 ½ lb. ground turkey

1 tsp salt

Sliced cheese to taste

DIRECTIONS

1. Beat eggs in a bowl and add breadcrumbs and milk. Stir and mix.
2. Sprinkle the pepper, garlic, salt, seasoning and powdered onion.
3. Add turkey into the mixture and stir and mix well.
4. Create 5 oz burgers. Dent the center of each burger the size of a coin.
5. Add some cooking spray to the frying basket and drop the burgers.
6. Seal the air fryer lid and choose to fry at 400 F for 9 minutes.
7. If you would like to add cheese, after the burgers are done, place the cheese onto the burgers and air fry for 1 minute more.
8. Serve the burgers while still warm.

AIR FRYER TURKEY SKEWERS

Prep Time: 20 min   **Servings:** 6   **Kcal:** 56

INGREDIENTS

1 turkey breast

1 tbsp butter

1 tsp lime juice

1 tsp dried dill

Salt and pepper to taste

1 cup pineapple cubes

1 tbsp soy sauce

1 pinch cinnamon

1 tsp dried thyme

DIRECTIONS

1. Cut the turkey breasts into small cubes.
2. Combine the salt, pepper, soy sauce, lime juice, dill, thyme and cinnamon.
3. Coat the turkey cubes in it. Coat the pineapple in some salt, pepper and cinnamon.
4. Thread them into skewers. Add your air fryer basket in the instant pot.
5. Add the butter and place the skewers and put on duo crisp lid.
6. Air fry for 6 minutes and flip the skewers. Air fry for another 5 minutes. Serve.

COCONUT CRUSTED TURKEY BALLS

Prep Time: 20 min   **Servings:** 10   **Kcal:** 104

INGREDIENTS

- 1 cup minced turkey
- 1 tbsp olive oil
- 1 cup desiccated coconut
- ½ cup coconut flour
- Salt and pepper to taste
- ½ tsp mixed herbs
- 2 green chilies
- 1 egg, beaten
- 1 tsp garlic powder

DIRECTIONS

1. Mince the green chilies. Combine the green chilies, minced turkey, coconut flour, salt, pepper, egg, garlic, mixed herbs and mix well.
2. Use your hands and create little balls. Coat the balls in desiccated coconut.
3. Add the olive oil into your air fryer basket. Add the meatballs and add the dup crisp lid.
4. Air fry for 10 minutes and stir once. Air fry for another 8 minutes. Serve.

TURKEY SALAD

Prep Time: 10 min   **Servings:** 3   **Kcal:** 233

INGREDIENTS

- 1 turkey thighs, boneless
- Salt and pepper to taste
- 1 tsp paprika
- 1 tsp oil
- 1 cup kale
- 1 tbsp lime juice
- 1 tsp ginger powder
- 1 tbsp avocado oil
- 1 cup diced orange
- 1 tbsp apple cider vinegar
- 1 tsp garlic powder
- 1 tsp thyme, minced

DIRECTIONS

1. Cut the turkey thighs into small pieces.
2. In an instant pot, add the oil and the turkey pieces.
3. Cook on sauté mode with a sprinkle of garlic, ginger, paprika, salt and pepper.
4. Sauté for 8 minutes. Transfer them onto a mixing bowl.
5. Add the kale, orange, avocado oil, thyme, apple cider vinegar, lime juice, and sprinkle some more salt and pepper.
6. Toss well and serve.

CRISPY TURKEY STRIPS

Prep Time: 10 min   **Servings:** 2   **Kcal:** 182

INGREDIENTS

1 turkey breast	2 tbsp coconut flour	1 egg
Salt and pepper to taste	1 tsp ginger powder	1 tsp garlic powder
1 tbsp oil	1 tsp dried rosemary	

DIRECTIONS

1. Cut the turkey breast into semi thick strips.
2. Combine the egg, coconut flour, ginger powder, rosemary, salt, pepper, garlic powder and mix well.
3. Coat the turkey strips into the mixture.
4. In an instant pot add the oil.
5. Add the turkey strips and air fry for 6 minutes.
6. Serve hot.

TURKEY STEW

Prep Time: 30 min   **Servings:** 4   **Kcal:** 384

INGREDIENTS

2 turkey breasts	1 cup onion, halved	1 cup celery, diced
Salt and pepper to taste	2 green chilies	3 garlic cloves
1 cup carrots, diced	1 tsp dried rosemary	1 tsp cumin
2 cup vegetable stock	1 cup coconut milk	10 cranberries

DIRECTIONS

1. Cut the turkey breasts into medium chunks.
2. In an instant pot, add the turkey, vegetable stock, garlic, onion, and cover.
3. Cook on high pressure mode for 20 minutes.
4. Add the carrot, celery, cranberries, coconut milk, salt, pepper, green chilies, rosemary and cover.
5. Cook on high pressure mode for another 10 minutes.
6. Release the pressure and serve hot.

TURKEY CASSEROLE

Prep Time: 60 min   **Servings:** 4   **Kcal:** 193

INGREDIENTS

1 turkey breast   2 eggs   1 cup flour

1 tsp garlic powder   1 tsp sage   Salt and pepper to taste

1 tsp dried mixed herbs 1 tsp chives, minced   ½ cup celery, diced

½ cup diced broccoli   ½ cup milk

DIRECTIONS

1. Chop the turkey breast finely.
2. Whisk the egg with the milk in a bowl.
3. Add the flour, garlic, salt, pepper, mixed herbs, sage and chives.
4. Add the turkey, broccoli and celery. Mix well.
5. Grease a baking dish and add the mixture.
6. Add the baking dish into your instant pot.
7. Cover and bake for 60 minutes. Let it rest for 10 minutes.
8. Serve warm.

LEFT-OVER TURKEY QUICHE

Prep Time: 20 min   **Servings:** 3   **Kcal:** 358

INGREDIENTS

1 cup left-over turkey	2 eggs	1 cup flour
1 tsp garlic powder	1 cup milk	Salt and pepper to taste
1 tsp dried oregano	1 tsp parsley, minced	½ cup scallion, diced
½ cup diced carrots	½ cup cheese, grated	

DIRECTIONS

1. In a bowl whisk the eggs for 1 minute.
2. Add the milk and mix well.
3. Add the salt, pepper, flour, oregano and garlic. Mix well.
4. Add the left-over turkey, cheese, scallions, and carrots. Mix well.
5. Add to a quiche dish and place it into your instant pot.
6. Cover and bake for 20 minutes. Serve hot.

CITRUS TURKEY ROAST

Prep Time: 80 min   **Servings:** 8   **Kcal:** 301

INGREDIENTS

- 1 whole turkey
- 6 garlic cloves
- 2 tbsp dried mixed herbs
- 2 tbsp paprika
- ½ cup butter
- ½ cup rice
- 1 cup diced potatoes
- 1 cup celery, diced
- 1 cup onion, sliced
- Salt and pepper to taste
- ½ cup orange juice

DIRECTIONS

1. Cut few slits onto the turkey.
2. Combine the mixed herbs, butter, salt, pepper, orange juice, paprika and mix well.
3. Rub the turkey using this mixture perfectly.
4. Combine the rice, potatoes, celery, onion, garlic and some salt and pepper.
5. Stuff the turkey with the mixture. Tie the legs using kitchen thread.
6. Add the turkey with its marinated juice in an instant pot.
7. Cover and roast for 80 minutes. Let it rest for 20 minutes.
8. Serve hot.

STUFFED SPINACH TURKEY BREASTS

Prep Time: 40 min   **Servings:** 2   **Kcal:** 303

INGREDIENTS

1 turkey breast

1 cup spinach, chopped

1 cup grated cheese

1 tsp garlic powder

½ cup chopped onion

Salt and pepper to taste

1 tsp dried mixed herbs

1 tsp chives, minced

1 tsp oil

1 tsp soy sauce

1 tsp paprika

DIRECTIONS

1. Remove the skin and bones of the turkey breast.
2. Use a kitchen hammer to flatten the turkey breast.
3. Add the spinach, onion, cheese and chives on the turkey breast.
4. Roll it tightly and use a kitchen thread to tie it.
5. In your instant pot, add the oil and place the turkey breast.
6. Sprinkle the mixed herbs, garlic powder, paprika, salt and pepper on top.
7. Add the soy sauce and turn on the roast mode.
8. Roast for 20 minutes and then flip it. Roast for 10 minutes and let it rest for 10 minutes.
9. Serve.

PORK RECIPES

SAUSAGE WITH ONIONS

Prep Time: 40 min   **Servings:** 4   **Kcal:** 700

INGREDIENTS

24 oz smoked sausage

3 diced onions

2 tsp olive oil

Salt to taste

Pepper to taste

DIRECTIONS

1. Select sauté mode and cook the onion with pepper and salt until browned.
2. Move the onion into the air frying basked and drop sausage in.
3. Apply air frying mode at 400 F for 28 minutes, mixing well every 3 minutes.
4. Serve warm.

GARLIC BREAD PIZZA

Prep Time: 20 min   **Servings:** 5   **Kcal:** 380

INGREDIENTS

10 slices frozen toast garlic bread

10 tbsp pizza sauce

4 oz peperoni

2 ½ cups shredded mozzarella

DIRECTIONS

1. Place all toasts into the air fryer basket and top each toast with pepperoni, sauce and cheese.
2. Seal the crisp lid and set the air fryer to 380 F for 6minutes.
3. Serve hot.

SAUSAGE BALLS

Prep Time: 20 min   **Servings:** 6   **Kcal:** 475

INGREDIENTS

1 lb. Sausage   1 lb. Velveeta cheese   1 ½ cups baking mix

DIRECTIONS

1. Preheat air fryer basket to 350F.
2. In a mixer, bring together the sausage and cheese.
3. Add baking mix and mix further a few times to make sure the mixture is well combined in the food processor.
4. Roll the mix into small size balls and place them inside the basket and seal the crisp lid.
5. Air fry for 5 minutes at 350 F.
6. Remove balls after opening the lid and flip them over. Seal the lid and air fry for further 5 minutes.

PORK CHOPS

Prep Time: 80 min   **Servings:** 4   **Kcal:** 293

INGREDIENTS

- 4 pork chops
- 1 tsp garlic paste
- 1 tsp ginger paste
- Salt to taste
- Pepper to taste
- 1 tbsp oil
- 2 tsp soy sauce
- 1 tsp lime juice
- 1 tsp paprika
- 1 tsp thyme, minced

DIRECTIONS

1. Combine the thyme, soy sauce, salt, lime juice, pepper, paprika, ginger and garlic in a bowl.
2. Marinate the pork chops using the mixture.
3. Let it sit for 1 hour or longer.
4. In your instant pot, add the oil. Place the pork chops.
5. Cover with lid and choose the roast option.
6. Roast for 10 minutes and flip the pork chops.
7. Roast for another 10 minutes. Let them rest for 10 minutes and then serve.

PORK FRIED RICE

Prep Time: 30 min   **Servings:** 4   **Kcal:** 669

INGREDIENTS

- 2 pork fillets
- 4 garlic cloves, minced
- 1 tbsp oil
- 1 tsp mixed herbs
- 3 cup long grain rice
- 1 tsp ginger, minced
- 1 tsp red chili powder
- 1 tsp rosemary, minced
- 2 white onion, sliced
- Salt and pepper to taste
- 1 tsp cumin

DIRECTIONS

1. Cut the pork fillets into thin slices.
2. In an instant pot, cook the 6 cups of water with high pressure mode.
3. Transfer the rice into a bowl.
4. In the instant pot, add the oil and sauté onion for 2 minutes.
5. Add the garlic, ginger, and the pork pieces.
6. Add salt, pepper, cumin, rosemary, mixed herbs and red chili powder.
7. Sauté for 5 minutes and add the rice. Stir for 5 minutes and then serve hot.

PORK STEW WITH VEGGIES

Prep Time: 3 hours   **Servings:** 4   **Kcal:** 378

INGREDIENTS

2 lb. pork

1 cup onion

1 cup potato

1 cup carrot

6 cup vegetable stock

Salt and pepper to taste

1 tsp cumin

1 tsp coriander

1 tsp garlic powder

1 tsp ginger powder

1 tsp sage

3 green chilies

DIRECTIONS

1. Cut the pork into medium chunks. Remove the bones and fat.
2. Cut the onion, carrot, potatoes in medium chunks.
3. In an instant pot, add the pork and sauté for 5 minutes.
4. Add the vegetable stock, ginger, garlic and cover.
5. Cook on slow cooking mode for 2 hours.
6. Add the vegetables, cumin, salt, pepper, green chilies, sage and coriander.
7. Cover and cook on slow cooking mode for another 1 hour.
8. Serve hot.

PORK BROCCOLI STIR FRY

Prep Time: 15 min   **Servings:** 2   **Kcal:** 451

INGREDIENTS

1 cup pork belly

4 garlic cloves, sliced

1 tbsp oil

½ tsp mixed herbs

1 ½ cup broccoli florets

1 tsp ginger powder

3 green chilies

1 white onion, sliced

Salt and pepper to taste

1 tsp parsley, chopped

DIRECTIONS

1. Cut the pork belly into thin slices.
2. Cut the broccoli florets into small pieces.
3. In an instant pot, add the oil and the onion and garlic.
4. Sauté for 1 minute and add the pork slices. Stir for 3 minutes.
5. Add the broccoli, mixed herbs, salt, parsley, pepper, ginger, green chilies and cover.
6. Cook for 8 minutes. Serve hot.

PORK CASHEW NUT SALAD

Prep Time: 15 min   **Servings:** 2   **Kcal:** 584

INGREDIENTS

1 pork fillet. sliced   1 cup cashew, toasted   Salt and pepper to taste

1 tbsp olive oil   1 tbsp soy sauce   1 tbsp lime juice

1 green chilies, chopped   1 tbsp scallion, chopped   1 cup diced capsicum

1 tsp mixed herbs   1 tsp parsley. chopped   1 egg

DIRECTIONS

1. Combine the mixed herbs, soy sauce, parsley, and lime juice in a container, shake well and set aside.
2. Whisk the egg with salt, pepper and add the pork slices in the mixture.
3. In an instant pot, add the pork pieces with olive oil and air fry until they become crispy.
4. In a mixing bowl, combine the capsicum, scallions, green chilies, cashews and pork pieces.
5. Add the dressing and toss well. Serve immediately.

PORK STEAK WITH CAULIFLOWER

Prep Time: 60 min   **Servings:** 2   **Kcal:** 299

INGREDIENTS

- 2 pork steak
- Salt and pepper to taste
- 1 tsp BBQ sauce
- 1 cup cauliflower florets, diced
- 1 tsp cumin
- 1 tsp paprika
- 1 tsp thyme, minced
- 1 tbsp butter
- 1 tsp lime juice
- 1 tbsp olive oil

DIRECTIONS

1. Marinate the pork with salt, cumin, pepper, BBQ sauce, lime juice and thyme.
2. Let it sit for 10 minutes.
3. In an instant pot, add the olive oil and place the pork steak.
4. Choose the roast option and roast for 20 minutes. Flip them and roast for 5 minutes.
5. Transfer to a serving plate.
6. Add the butter in the instant pot and choose the sauté mode.
7. Add the cauliflower, salt, pepper, paprika and toss for 6 minutes.
8. Serve the pork steak with butter tossed cauliflower.

GREEN BEAN PORK BITES

Prep Time: 15 min **Servings:** 2 **Kcal:** 206

INGREDIENTS

1 pork fillet

1 cup green beans

1 onion, sliced

4 garlic cloves, sliced

1 tbsp butter

1 tsp oregano

1 tsp thyme, minced

1 tbsp soy sauce

Salt and pepper to taste

DIRECTIONS

1. Cut the pork fillet into small cubes.
2. Cut the green beans in half.
3. In an instant pot, add the butter.
4. Add the pork and sauté for 5 minutes.
5. Add the green beans, onion and sauté for 2 minutes.
6. Add the soy sauce, thyme, garlic, pepper, salt, and oregano.
7. Sauté for 5 minutes and serve hot.

BEEF RECIPES

CRISPY CHUCK ROAST

Prep Time: 30 min   **Servings:** 4   **Kcal:** 550

INGREDIENTS

2 tbsp liquid smoke	3 cloves garlic	1/3 cup vinegar
2 lb. chuck roast	2 tsp salt & pepper	1 tbsp garlic powder
1 cup BBQ Sauce	1 tsp sugar	1 ½ tbsp honey

DIRECTIONS

1. Drop garlic powder, pepper and salt over the chuck roast and rib the seasoning onto the meat.
2. Add into the pot the crushed garlic, vinegar and liquid smoke.
3. Place the meant into the pot and lock pressure lid. Cook on high for 5 minutes.
4. Release pressure and let it rest for 12 minutes.
5. Mix on a bow the BBQ sauce, sugar and honey and mix well.
6. Remove meat from pot and mix well with the mixture in the bowl.
7. Place the trivet into the pot and put a crisp lid basket on top.
8. Put the meat onto the basket.
9. Please the lid on the pot and select 300 F for 10 minutes, flipping the meat after 5.
10. Open the lid and add some more sauce and drop a bit more sugar.
11. Time now to 450 F for 10 minutes. Remove meat.

CRISPY POT ROAST

Prep Time: 100 min   **Servings:** 5   **Kcal:** 600

INGREDIENTS

3 lb. chuck roast

2 tsp garlic powder

Salt and pepper

2 lb. baby potatoes

1 ½ lb. baby carrots

Decoration herbs to taste

DIRECTIONS

1. Drop the roast together with water into the instant pot. With a trivet, keep the roast above the liquid. You may use Mealthy Crisp Lid.
2. Close the pressure lid and set to high pressure for 60 minutes.
3. After applying the quick pressure release, drop the carrots and potatoes and set to high for 8 further minutes.
4. Apply a natural release for 7 minutes and remove the lid.
5. Air fry for 7 minutes at 400 F.
6. Serve warm.

RIBEYE STEAK

Prep Time: 12 min   **Servings:** 1   **Kcal:** 192

INGREDIENTS

1 rib-eye beef steak	½ tsp dried oregano	1 tsp lime juice
1 tsp butter	Salt and pepper to taste	½ tsp garlic powder
½ tsp honey	1 tsp onion paste	½ tsp chili flakes

DIRECTIONS

1. Marinate the steak using lime juice, honey, salt, pepper, garlic, onion, oregano and chili flakes.
2. In your instant pot, add an air fryer basket. Add the butter. Add the steak.
3. Add the duo crisp lid and air fry for 6 minutes.
4. Flip the steak and air fry for another 5 minutes.
5. Serve after resting for 10 minutes.

DUO CRISP STEAK BITES

Prep Time: 10 min **Servings:** 1 **Kcal:** 232

INGREDIENTS

- 1 beef steak
- 1 tsp butter
- 1 tsp red chili powder
- ½ tsp dried thyme
- Salt and pepper to taste
- 1 tsp honey
- ½ tsp dried dill
- ½ tsp garlic powder
- ½ tsp ginger powder

DIRECTIONS

1. Cut the beef steak into bite size pieces.
2. Marinate the beef steak pieces using honey, salt, dill, pepper, thyme, ginger, garlic and red chili powder.
3. In your instant pot, place the air fryer basket.
4. Add the butter and place the steak bites.
5. Add the duo crisp lid and air fry for 5 minutes.
6. Give it one stir and air fry for another 4 minutes. Serve.

BEEF BROCCOLI STIR FRY

Prep Time: 12 min   **Servings:** 2   **Kcal:** 340

INGREDIENTS

1 cup beef, sliced thinly   1 cup broccoli, diced   Salt and pepper to taste

1 white onion, sliced   3 garlic cloves, sliced   ½ tsp oregano

2 green chilies   1 tbsp butter   10 cashews

DIRECTIONS

1. In an instant pot, add the butter.
2. Add the beef slices and sauté for 3 minutes.
3. Add the onion, garlic, and sauté for 2 minutes.
4. Add the green chilies, salt, pepper, oregano, and cashew.
5. Sauté for 6 minutes. Serve hot.

MINCED BEEF RICE

Prep Time: 25 min   **Servings:** 2   **Kcal:** 487

INGREDIENTS

- 1 cup minced beef
- 1 tsp minced ginger
- Pepper to taste
- 2 green chilies
- 1 cup rice
- 1 tsp minced garlic
- 1 tsp chives
- 3 cup water
- 1 tsp mixed herbs
- Salt to taste
- 1 tbsp oil
- 1 tbsp lime juice

DIRECTIONS

1. In an instant pot, add the oil and sauté the minced beef until they are brown.
2. Add the rice, ginger, garlic, green chilies, lime juice, mixed herbs, salt, pepper, and water.
3. Cover and cook on high pressure mode for 20 minutes.
4. Release the pressure and serve with chives on top.

BEEF CURRY

Prep Time: 40 min   **Servings:** 4   **Kcal:** 505

INGREDIENTS

2 lb. beef

Salt and pepper to taste

1 tbsp oil

1 tsp cumin

1 cup potatoes, diced

4 cup beef stock

1 tbsp paprika

1 tbsp scallion, chopped

1 tsp garlic paste

1 tsp ginger paste

½ tsp turmeric

1 tsp coriander

DIRECTIONS

1. Cut the beef into medium chunks.
2. In an instant pot, add the oil and sauté the beef for 5 minutes.
3. Add the ginger, garlic, paprika, cumin, turmeric, coriander, salt, pepper and sauté for 5 minutes.
4. Pour in the beef stock.
5. Cover and cook with high pressure mode for 40 minutes.
6. Add the scallions on top and serve hot.

BEEF MEATBALL

Prep Time: 20 min   **Servings:** 3   **Kcal:** 277

INGREDIENTS

- 2 cup minced beef
- 1 tsp minced ginger
- Salt and pepper to taste
- 2 green chilies, chopped
- ½ cup corn flour
- 1 tsp minced garlic
- 1 tsp chives
- ½ tsp cumin
- 1 egg
- 1 cup tomato puree
- 1 tsp chili flakes
- 1 tsp paprika
- 1 tbsp olive oil

DIRECTIONS

1. In a bowl, combine the minced beef, egg, corn flour, salt, green chilies, pepper and mix well.
2. Use your hands to make meatballs.
3. In an instant pot, add half of the oil and air fry the meatballs for 5 minutes.
4. Take the meatballs out and place on a serving dish.
5. Add the remaining oil in the instant pot.
6. Add the garlic, ginger and sauté for 1 minute.
7. Add the tomato puree, chili flakes, paprika, salt, pepper, cumin, and chives.
8. Cover and cook for 5 minutes.
9. Pour the sauce on top of the meatballs and serve.

BEEF STEAK

Prep Time: 80 min **Servings:** 1 **Kcal:** 217

INGREDIENTS

1 beef steak

1 tsp BBQ sauce

½ tsp parsley, chopped

1 tsp ginger powder

1 tsp minced garlic

1 tsp lime juice

Salt to taste

1 tsp sage

Pepper to taste

1 tsp butter

½ tsp paprika

DIRECTIONS

1. Combine the ginger, garlic, sage, salt, BBQ sauce, paprika, pepper, lime juice and marinate the steak in it for 1 hour.
2. In an instant pot add the butter.
3. Add the beef steak and bake for 10 minutes.
4. Flip the steak and bake for 5 minutes.
5. Serve hot with parsley on top.

BEEF CARROT STEW

Prep Time: 30 min   **Servings:** 2   **Kcal:** 167

INGREDIENTS

1 cup beef	1 tsp red chili powder	1 cup onion, halved
Salt to taste	1 tsp minced garlic	1 tsp minced ginger
1 tsp cumin	½ tsp turmeric	Pepper to taste
1 tsp rosemary, minced	1 cup carrots, cut into chunks	3 cup beef stock

DIRECTIONS

1. Remove the bones and cut the beef into medium chunks.
2. In an instant pot, add the beef with the beef stock.
3. Cover and cook on high pressure mode for 15 minutes.
4. Add the carrots, onion, cumin, turmeric, rosemary, red chili powder, salt, pepper, ginger and garlic.
5. Stir and cover. Cook for another 10 minutes.
6. Serve hot.

BEEF PASTA

Prep Time: 20 min   **Servings:** 2   **Kcal:** 523

INGREDIENTS

- 1 cup minced beef
- 1 tsp minced ginger
- Pepper to taste
- 1 cup water
- 1 cup pasta
- 1 tsp minced garlic
- 1 tsp chives, chopped
- ½ tsp oregano
- 1 red onion, sliced
- Salt to taste
- 1 tbsp butter
- 4 tbsp parmesan cheese, grated

DIRECTIONS

1. In an instant pot, add the butter and toss the minced beef for 3 minutes.
2. Add the ginger, garlic, and onion. Sauté for 3 minutes.
3. Add the pasta, water, chives, oregano, salt, pepper, and cook for 8 minutes.
4. Add the cheese and cook for 3 minutes.
5. Serve hot.

LAMB RECIPES

ASIAN FRIED LAMB CHOPS

Prep Time: 60 min   **Servings:** 8   **Kcal:** 730

INGREDIENTS

- 2 ½ lamb chops
- 2 oz soya sauce
- 3 tsp pepper paste
- 1 tbsp sesame oil
- 1 tsp black pepper
- 3 cups water
- 2 bay leaves
- Cilantro to taste
- 3 tsp sugar
- 1 oz cooking wine
- 3 tsp ketchup
- 1 tsp cinnamon
- ½ cup powdered onion
- 1 cup red wine
- 3 cups sliced onion
- Green onions to taste
- 1 ½ tbsp curry powder
- 3 tbsp chopped garlic
- 1 oz corn syrup
- 2 tsp sesame seeds
- 1 tsp plum extract
- 1 ½ cups carrots
- 1 ½ cups celery

DIRECTIONS

1. Drop all ingredients but green onions and cilantro to the pot and close the lid.
2. Select pressure to high and let it cook for 18 minutes.
3. Apply a natural release of the pressure for 12 minutes and remove the lamb.
4. Select sauté mode to thicken the sauce while stirring. Do this for 3 minutes.
5. Drop the resulting sauce into a separate bowl. Wash the inside of the pot afterwards.
6. Cut the chops and place them on the dehydration rack before placing them into the air fryer basket. Fix the air fryer lid.
7. Apply frying at 400F for 6 minutes and remove the chops. Do this process for all the chops.
8. Serve with cilantro and green onions as decoration.

LAMB SKEWERS

Prep Time: 15 min **Servings:** 8 **Kcal:** 48

INGREDIENTS

1 lamb steak

1 tbsp olive oil

1 pinch sage

1 cup onion, halved

Salt and pepper to taste

1 cup bell pepper, diced

1 tbsp soy sauce

1 tsp garlic powder

½ tsp mixed herbs

DIRECTIONS

1. Cut the lamb steak into bite size pieces.
2. Use toothpicks to thread the steak pieces, bell pepper, and onion.
3. Sprinkle the salt, pepper, garlic powder, mixed herbs, sage and add soy sauce.
4. In your instant pot, add the air fryer basket. Add the olive oil.
5. Place the skewers and add the duo crisp lid. Air fry for 6 minutes.
6. Turn them over and air fry for another 5 minutes. Serve.

HONEY LAMB CHOPS

Prep Time: 90 min   **Servings:** 6   **Kcal:** 192

INGREDIENTS

6 lamb chops

1 tsp dried oregano

1 tbsp soy sauce

1 tbsp honey

Salt and pepper to taste

1 tsp garlic powder

1 tsp rosemary, minced

1 tsp red chili powder

1 tbsp butter

DIRECTIONS

1. Combine the soy sauce, honey, rosemary, garlic, red chili powder, salt and pepper. Mix well.
2. Marinate the lamb chops in the mixture and let it sit for 1 hour.
3. In your instant pot, place the air fryer basket and add the butter.
4. Place the lamb chops and put on the dup crisp lid on.
5. Air fry for 10 minutes and flip the lamb chops.
6. Air fry for another 10 minutes. Let it rest for 10 minutes and then serve warm.

GARLIC HONEY LAMB CHOPS

Prep Time: 50 min **Servings:** 2 **Kcal:** 232

INGREDIENTS

- 2 lamb chops
- 1 tsp soy sauce
- 1 tsp paprika
- 1 tsp minced ginger
- 1 tsp minced garlic
- 1 tsp honey
- Pepper to taste
- 1 tbsp butter
- Salt to taste
- ½ tsp sage
- ½ tsp cumin
- ½ oregano

DIRECTIONS

1. Combine the sage, cumin, soy sauce, salt, oregano, honey, paprika, garlic, pepper and ginger in a bowl.
2. Add the lamb chops and marinate for 30 minutes.
3. In your instant pot, add the butter.
4. Add the marinated lamb chops and bake for 10 minutes.
5. Turn the lamb chops over and bake for another 10 minutes. Serve.

BELL PEPPER LAMB STIR FRY

Prep Time: 15 min   **Servings:** 2   **Kcal:** 171

INGREDIENTS

1 cup minced lamb   1 cup bell pepper, diced   ½ cup onion, chopped

1 tsp minced ginger   1 tsp minced garlic   1 tsp paprika

Pepper to taste   1 tsp chives   Sea salt to taste

1 tbsp butter   ½ tsp thyme   2 green chilies

DIRECTIONS

1. In an instant pot, melt the butter.
2. Add the minced lamb and sauté for 4 minutes.
3. Add the onion, ginger, garlic and sauté for 3 minutes.
4. Add the sea salt, pepper, thyme, chives, green chilies, paprika and sauté for 2 minutes.
5. Add the bell pepper and cook for 3 minutes. Serve hot.

CHICKPEA LAMB STEW

Prep Time: 60 min   **Servings:** 6   **Kcal:** 449

INGREDIENTS

- 2 lb. lamb
- 1 tsp chili flakes
- Salt to taste
- 2 green chilies
- 1 cup chickpeas, boiled
- 1 tsp minced garlic
- 1 tsp coriander
- 1 tsp cumin
- 1 cup lamb stock
- 1 tsp minced ginger
- Pepper to taste
- ½ tsp turmeric

DIRECTIONS

1. Cut the lamb into small chunks.
2. In an instant pot, add the lamb with the lamb stock.
3. Cover and cook on high pressure mode for 30 minutes.
4. Add the chickpeas, green chilies, salt, coriander, cumin, turmeric, pepper, ginger, garlic and chili flakes.
5. Cover and cook for 30 minutes in slow cooking mode. Serve hot.

LAMB SHANK

Prep Time: 3 hours   **Servings:** 1   **Kcal:** 531

INGREDIENTS

1 lamb shank

1 tsp lime juice

1 pinch turmeric

1 tsp ginger paste

1 tsp garlic paste

1 tsp chili flakes

Pepper to taste

1 tsp thyme

Sea salt to taste

1 cup lamb stock

1 tbsp butter

1 tsp smoked paprika

DIRECTIONS

1. Combine the lime juice, salt, ginger, pepper, garlic, thyme, turmeric, smoked paprika, chili flakes, and mix well.
2. Add the lamb shank and marinate for 1 hour.
3. In your instant pot, add the butter and bake the lamb shank for 20 minutes.
4. Add the lamb stock and slow cook for 2 hours. Serve hot.

ROSEMARY LAMB LEG ROAST

Prep Time: 2 hours   **Servings:** 4   **Kcal:** 261

INGREDIENTS

- 2 lamb legs
- 1 tbsp oil
- 1 tsp garlic paste
- 1 tsp rosemary
- 1 tbsp lime juice
- 1 tsp ginger paste
- Salt and pepper to taste
- 4 tbsp yogurt
- 1 tsp red chili powder

DIRECTIONS

1. Combine the yogurt, red chili powder, garlic, ginger, salt, pepper, lime juice and rosemary in a bowl.
2. Add the lamb legs and marinate for 1 hour.
3. In an instant pot, add the oil.
4. Add the lamb leg with its yogurt.
5. Cover and cook on roast mode for 1 hour. Serve hot.

VEGETARIAN RECIPES

MAC & CHEESE

Prep Time: 25 min   **Servings:** 4   **Kcal:** 475

INGREDIENTS

- 3 Cups macaroni
- 3 cups vegetable stock
- 2 cups heavy cream
- 7 tbsp butter
- 3 cups shredded cheddar
- ½ cup parmesan
- 1 tsp garlic powder
- Salt to taste
- Pepper to taste

DIRECTIONS

1. Drop chicken stock, heavy cream and water into the instant pot and mix well.
2. Drop the macaroni and close the pressure-cooking lid.
3. Set on high pressure mode for 5 minutes.
4. Apply quick pressure release.
5. Drop the cups of cheese and wait until it melts.
6. Seal the air frying crisp lid and set to 400 F for 6 minutes.
7. Serve warm.

SOY SAUCE CAULIFLOWER

Prep Time: 20 min **Servings:** 6 **Kcal:** 475

INGREDIENTS

6 cups chopped cauliflower

½ cup soy sauce

2 tsp oil

3 tsp garlic powder

1 tbsp flour

Salt to taste

DIRECTIONS

1. Drop in a bowl the sauce, oil, garlic powder, cauliflower, flour and salt and mix well.
2. Add cooking stir to the air fryer grill and cover with crisping lid.
3. Set to 400 F for 18 min. After 9 minutes flip the cauliflower.
4. Remove from air fryer and serve warm.

PESTO VEGGIE PASTA

Prep Time: 10 min   **Servings:** 2   **Kcal:** 269

INGREDIENTS

1 cup pasta

1 onion, diced

2 garlic cloves, sliced

1 tsp ginger, sliced

1 tsp paprika

1 tsp oregano

Pepper to taste

1 tsp soy sauce

Salt to taste

½ cup grated carrot

1 tbsp pesto

1 cup vegetable stock

DIRECTIONS

1. In an instant pot, add the vegetable stock with the garlic, ginger and onion.
2. Add the pasta, salt, pepper, carrot, pesto, oregano, soy sauce, and paprika.
3. Cover and cook on high pressure mode for 8 minutes.
4. Serve hot.

EGGPLANT IN TOMATO GRAVY

Prep Time: 15 min   **Servings:** 2   **Kcal:** 150

INGREDIENTS

1 large eggplant	2 tbsp tamarind pulp	1 tbsp tomato puree
1 tsp ginger paste	1 tsp chili flakes	1 tsp garlic paste
Pepper to taste	1 tsp cumin	Salt to taste
1 tbsp oil	1 tsp mixed herbs	½ cup vegetable stock

DIRECTIONS

1. Cut the eggplant in half and coat it with salt, pepper, and cumin.
2. In an instant pot, add the oil and sauté the eggplant until brown.
3. Take out the eggplant and add the chili flakes, ginger, garlic, tamarind pulp, tomato puree, vegetable stock, salt, pepper and mixed herbs.
4. Cook for 5 minutes and add the eggplant in the instant pot.
5. Cover and cook for 8 minutes. Serve hot.

STUFFED ZUCCHINI

Prep Time: 15 min   **Servings:** 2   **Kcal:** 176

INGREDIENTS

- 2 zucchinis
- ½ tsp paprika
- Pepper to taste
- ½ tsp parsley, chopped
- 1 tbsp olive oil
- 2 garlic cloves, minced
- 1 onion, chopped
- 1 cup mushroom, chopped
- 1 tomato, chopped
- 1 tsp mixed herbs
- Salt to taste
- 1 cup Vegan cheddar cheese, grated

DIRECTIONS

1. Cut the zucchinis in half and scoop out the flesh to make pockets inside.
2. In an instant pot, add the oil and sauté the onion, garlic, for 1 minute.
3. Add the mushroom, salt, pepper and sauté for 1 minute.
4. Take them out and combine with parsley, mixed herbs, tomato, paprika and stuff the zucchinis.
5. Add the vegan cheese on top.
6. Place them onto the instant pot and bake for 10 minutes.
7. Serve hot.

AIRFRIED PLANTAIN CHIPS

Prep Time: 10 min   **Servings:** 4   **Kcal:** 139

INGREDIENTS

2 plantains	1 tsp paprika	½ tsp sage
2 tbsp rice flour	Salt to taste	1 tsp oil

DIRECTIONS

1. Peel the plantains and cut then into thin slices.
2. Coat them in salt, paprika, sage and rice flour.
3. In an instant pot add the oil.
4. Place the plantain slices and air fry for 10 minutes.
5. Serve hot.

STUFFED BELL PEPPER

Prep Time: 50 min   **Servings:** 2   **Kcal:** 174

INGREDIENTS

- 2 bell peppers
- 1 cup tofu, crumbled
- 1 cup mushroom, sliced
- ½ cup tomatoes, chopped
- 1 tsp ginger, minced
- 1 tsp garlic, minced
- Salt to taste
- Pepper to taste
- 1 tsp mixed herbs
- 1 onion, chopped
- 1 tbsp soy sauce

DIRECTIONS

1. Cut the stem off the bell peppers.
2. Make pockets inside by scooping out the flesh from inside.
3. Combine the tomatoes, garlic, ginger, mushroom, salt, pepper, mixed herbs, soy sauce and onion in a bowl.
4. Stuff the bell peppers using the mixture.
5. Place the bell peppers into your instant pot.
6. Sprinkle the crumbled tofu on top.
7. Roast for 40 minutes. Serve hot.

TOFU CAULIFLOWER STIR FRY

Prep Time: 15 min   **Servings:** 2   **Kcal:** 194

INGREDIENTS

- 1 cup tofu, cut into cubes
- 1 cup cauliflower florets
- Salt to taste
- 1 tsp soy sauce
- 1 tbsp coriander, chopped
- 1 onion, chopped
- 1 tsp mixed herbs
- 2 green chilies
- 1 pinch thyme
- 3 garlic cloves, minced
- Pepper to taste
- 1 tbsp oil

DIRECTIONS

1. In an instant pot, add the oil with the onion and garlic.
2. Sauté for 1 minute and then add the tofu.
3. Sauté until they are golden.
4. Add the cauliflower, salt, pepper, mixed herbs, green chilies, thyme, coriander, soy sauce and sauté for 5 minutes. Serve hot.

BROCCOLI QUINOA FRY

Prep Time: 20 min   **Servings:** 2   **Kcal:** 400

INGREDIENTS

1 cup broccoli florets, diced	1 cup quinoa	1 tbsp oil
1 tsp mixed herbs	1 tsp garlic, minced	1 tsp ginger, minced
Pepper to taste	Salt to taste	1 tsp paprika
1 tsp rosemary, minced	1 tsp chives, chopped	1 cup water

DIRECTIONS

1. In an instant pot, add the oil and sauté the quinoa and broccoli for 2 minutes.
2. Add the water, mixed herbs, rosemary, salt, pepper, chives, paprika, ginger and garlic.
3. Cook on high pressure mode for 8 minutes.
4. Release the pressure and serve hot.

SPINACH LENTIL CURRY

Prep Time: 15 min   **Servings:** 2   **Kcal:** 377

INGREDIENTS

1 cup lentil	1 cup spinach	½ cup water
1 tsp ginger paste	1 tsp paprika	1 tsp garlic
Pepper to taste	1 onion, chopped	Salt to taste
1 tsp coriander, chopped	1 tsp cumin	1 tsp coriander powder

DIRECTIONS

1. In an instant pot add the lentil with garlic, ginger, onion and water.
2. Cook with high pressure mode for 10 minutes.
3. Add the spinach, coriander powder, cumin, salt, pepper, and paprika.
4. Cook for 5 minutes and take off the instant pot.
5. Serve hot with coriander leaves on top.

CAULIFLOWER SOUP

Prep Time: 15 min   **Servings:** 2   **Kcal:** 178

INGREDIENTS

- 1 cup cauliflower florets, diced
- 1 cup vegetable stock
- ½ cup coconut cream
- 1 tsp chives, chopped
- ½ tsp ginger powder
- 1 tsp chili flakes
- Salt to taste
- Pepper to taste
- 1 pinch sage
- 1 tsp oil
- ½ tsp oregano
- 2 tbsp celery, diced

DIRECTIONS

1. In an instant pot, add the oil and toss the cauliflower for 2 minutes.
2. Add the vegetable stock, salt, pepper, oregano, coconut cream, celery, chili flakes, sage, and chives.
3. Cover and cook on high pressure mode for 10 minutes.
4. Serve hot.

DESSERT RECIPES

COATED APPLE CHIPS

Prep Time: 20 min **Servings:** 4 **Kcal:** 218

INGREDIENTS

2 apples

1 tbsp butter

1 cup dry coconut

4 tsp honey

1 pinch Sea salt

½ tsp cinnamon

1 tbsp chopped walnuts

½ cup breadcrumbs

½ tsp cardamom

DIRECTIONS

1. Cut the apples into thick sticks. In a bowl, combine the honey, cardamom, cinnamon, and sea salt. Roll the apple sticks into the mixture.
2. Combine the breadcrumbs, walnuts and coconut in a plate.
3. Coat the apple sticks in the honey mix and roll them into the walnut mix.
4. Place an air fryer basket into the instant pot.
5. Add the butter and place the apple sticks.
6. Add the dup crisp lid and air fry for 8 minutes.
7. Stir them once and air fry for another 6 minutes.
8. Serve at room temperature.

AIR FRYER BREAD STICKS

Prep Time: 10 min   **Servings:** 6   **Kcal:** 372

INGREDIENTS

- 4 eggs, beaten
- ½ cup butter
- 1 cup dry coconut
- 1 cup bread, cubed
- ½ cup heavy milk
- 1 pinch cinnamon
- ½ cup breadcrumbs
- ½ cup sugar

DIRECTIONS

1. Combine the heavy milk with the eggs. Add the cinnamon sugar and mix well.
2. In a plate combine the breadcrumbs and coconut and mix well.
3. Dip the bread cubes into the egg mix first and then roll into the breadcrumb mix.
4. Place the air fryer basket in your instant pot. Add the butter and add the bread cubes. Add the duo crisp lid and air fry for 5 minutes.
5. Stir once gently and air fry for another 5 minutes.
6. Serve at room temperature.

EGG FLAN

Prep Time: 60 min   **Servings:** 4   **Kcal:** 170

INGREDIENTS

1 cup heavy milk

1 tsp butter

1 tsp vanilla extract

3 eggs

2 tbsp brown sugar

½ cup sugar

1 pinch cinnamon powder

DIRECTIONS

1. Whisk the eggs in a bowl.
2. Run the egg mix through a sieve.
3. Add the heavy milk, sugar, vanilla and cinnamon. Mix well.
4. In a pot, add the butter and the brown sugar.
5. Add to the instant pot and cook until it becomes caramelized.
6. Take it out and let it cool down completely.
7. Pour in the egg mixture.
8. Add 1 cup of water in your instant pot. Place a trivet and add the flan pot.
9. Cover and pressure cook for 20 minutes.
10. Release the pressure and serve the flan cold.

CHOCOLATE MUFFIN

Prep Time: 15 min   **Servings:** 8   **Kcal:** 350

INGREDIENTS

1 cup dark chocolate, melted

1 pinch salt

2/3 cup sugar

½ cup butter, soften

1 cup flour

2 eggs

1 tsp white vinegar

1 tsp baking powder

1 tsp chocolate extract

¼ tsp baking soda

DIRECTIONS

1. Shift the flour, baking powder, baking soda and salt.
2. In a bowl beat the eggs with the sugar.
3. Add the butter, chocolate extract, white vinegar, and melted chocolate.
4. Beat well and pour into a prepared muffin pan.
5. In your instant pot, add the muffin tray.
6. Cover and bake for 10 minutes.
7. Serve at room temperature.

RICE PUDDING

Prep Time: 2 hours **Servings:** 2 **Kcal:** 483

INGREDIENTS

½ cup rice

1 cardamom

1 pinch salt

2 cup milk

1 bay leaf

½ cup sugar

1 tsp cinnamon powder

1 tsp corn flour

DIRECTIONS

1. In a bowl combine the milk, rice, sugar, cardamom, bay leaf, cinnamon and corn flour.
2. Stir until well combined and add the mixture into an instant pot.
3. Cover and cook on slow cooker mode for 1 hour.
4. Let it cool down completely and then refrigerate for 1 hour. Serve.

MANGO COCONUT RICE PUDDING

Prep Time: 15 min **Servings:** 4 **Kcal:** 502

INGREDIENTS

½ cup rice

1 cardamom

1 pinch salt

2 cup coconut milk

1 bay leaf

½ cup shredded coconut

½ cup mango puree

½ cup sugar

2 tbsp mango cubes, to serve

DIRECTIONS

1. In a bowl, mix the coconut milk, sugar and mango puree.
2. Add the bay leaf, cardamom, salt and shredded coconut.
3. Add the mixture into an instant pot.
4. Cover and pressure cook for 10 minutes.
5. Let it cool down completely.
6. Add the mango cubes on top and serve.

ALMOND CAKE

Prep Time: 40 min   **Servings:** 8   **Kcal:** 158

INGREDIENTS

1 cup almond flour

½ cup chopped almonds

2/3 cup sugar

3 eggs

1 tsp almond extract

1 pinch salt

½ cup almond butter

¼ tsp baking soda

1 tsp baking powder

2 tbsp almond milk

DIRECTIONS

1. Shift the dry ingredients in a bowl.
2. In another bowl combine the sugar and eggs and beat well.
3. Add the butter, milk, almond extract, and beat again.
4. Shift in the dry ingredients, chopped almonds and fold in using a spoon.
5. Prepare a cake pan and pour the batter.
6. In your instant pot, add the cake pan and bake for 30 minutes.
7. Serve in room temperature.

BROWNIE

Prep Time: 40 min   **Servings:** 8   Kcal: 404

INGREDIENTS

1 cup chocolate, melted   1 tsp salt   1 egg

3 tbsp milk   1 tsp vanilla extract   1 cup butter

1 tsp baking powder   ½ cup sugar   ½ cup flour

DIRECTIONS

1. Shift the flour, salt, and baking powder in a bowl.
2. Beat the egg and sugar in a bowl.
3. Add the milk, butter, vanilla and beat for 3 minutes.
4. Add the shifted dry ingredients.
5. Mix using a spatula and pour in a prepared square pan.
6. Add to an instant pot and bake for 30 minutes.
7. Serve warm or in room temperature.

CARROT CAKE

Prep Time: 50 min   **Servings:** 8   **Kcal:** 330

INGREDIENTS

1 cup butter

1 egg

½ cup grated carrot

½ tsp nutmeg

1 cup flour

½ cup sugar

1 pinch salt

½ cup yogurt

1 tsp baking powder

1 tsp cinnamon powder

¼ tsp baking soda

DIRECTIONS

1. Shift the dry ingredients in a bowl. Set aside for now.
2. In a bowl whisk the egg.
3. Add the yogurt, butter and sugar and beat well.
4. Add the dry ingredients and fold in with a spoon.
5. Add the grated carrot and fold again.
6. Pour the mix into a prepared cake pan.
7. Add it to your instant pot and bake for 40 minutes.
8. Serve in room temperature.

FISH & SEAFOOD

SHRIMP TACOS

Prep Time: 30 min **Servings:** 5 **Kcal:** 300

INGREDIENTS

2 tbsp vegetable oil	30 peeled shrimps	2 tsp brown sugar
1 ½ tsp chili powder	1 tsp paprika	1 tsp garlic powder
1 tsp salt	1 cup diced avocado	1 cup purple cabbage
2/3 cup green salsa	2/3 cup sour cream	1/3 cup red onion
15 flour tortillas	Lime wedges	

DIRECTIONS

1. Brush the air frying basket with vegetable oil and preheat to 390F.
2. Stir brown sugar, paprika, garlic powder, chili powder and salt.
3. Mix the shrimp with the seasoning in a plastic bag, shaking it well.
4. Place the shrimp in the air fryer basket. Cook at 390F 5 min each side (flip the shrimps)
5. Mix salsa and sour cream to create the sauce.
6. Serve the rest of the ingredients wrapped in tacos.

ZESTY FISH FILETS

Prep Time: 10 min   **Servings:** 5   **Kcal:** 275

INGREDIENTS

1 cup breadcrumbs

2 beaten eggs

1 oz dry ranch dressing mix

5 tilapia filets

3 tbsp vegetable oil

Lemon wedges

DIRECTIONS

1. Preheat the air fryer basket to 350 F.
2. Mix the breadcrumbs and the dressing. Add the oil and mix well until the mixture is quite crumbly and loose.
3. Dip the fillets into the beaten egg.
4. Dip the wet fillets into the breadcrumb mix, coating well.
5. Drop into the air fryer basket and air fry for 14 minutes.
6. Open the lid and remove filets. Squeeze some lemon wedges all over and serve.

DUO CRISP TILAPIA FRY

Prep Time: 10 min   **Servings:** 4   **Kcal:** 257

INGREDIENTS

1 lb. tilapia

1 tbsp olive oil

½ cup coconut flour

½ tsp dried oregano

Salt and pepper to taste

1 egg, beaten

1 tbsp soy sauce

1 tsp garlic powder

½ cup breadcrumbs

DIRECTIONS

1. Clean the tilapia and marinate it using salt, pepper, oregano, soy sauce and garlic.
2. Combine the coconut flour, egg, salt and pepper. Dip the fish into the egg mix and coat in the breadcrumbs.
3. Place the air fryer basket into the instant pot. Add the olive oil and then place the tilapia carefully.
4. Add the duo crisp lid and air fry for 5 minutes. Turn the fish over and air fry for 4 minutes.
5. Serve.

HERB SALMON

Prep Time: 10 min **Servings:** 2 **Kcal:** 302

INGREDIENTS

2 salmon fillets

½ tsp dried oregano

1/2 tsp paprika

1 tbsp olive oil

Salt and pepper to taste

1 tsp garlic paste

½ tsp parsley, minced

1 tsp dill, minced

½ tsp onion paste

DIRECTIONS

1. Combine the garlic, dill, parsley, onion paste, garlic paste, salt, pepper, oregano and paprika. Let it sit for 5 minutes.
2. Place the air fryer basket into your instant pot.
3. Add your olive oil and place the herb crusted salmons.
4. Add the duo crisp lid and air fry for 5 minutes. Turn the salmon over and air fry for another 5 minutes.
5. Serve.

BAKED SALMON

Prep Time: 15 min   **Servings:** 2   **Kcal:** 261

INGREDIENTS

2 salmon fillets	Salt to taste	1 tsp oregano
½ tsp ginger paste	Black pepper to taste	1 tsp paprika
½ tsp garlic paste	1 tsp olive oil	1 tbsp lime juice

DIRECTIONS

1. Add the olive oil into your instant pot.
2. Marinate the salmon with ginger, garlic, lime juice, salt, black pepper, paprika and oregano.
3. Let it sit for 10 minutes. Add the salmon fillets into the instant pot.
4. Cover and bake the salmon for 15 minutes.
5. Serve hot.

FISH SOUP

Prep Time: 20 min   **Servings:** 2   **Kcal:** 452

INGREDIENTS

1 salmon fillet

½ cup oyster

1 cup fish stock

1 red chili

Salt and pepper to taste

1 tsp paprika

1 tsp ginger, sliced

½ cup medium shrimp

1 cup coconut milk

1 tsp lemongrass, chopped

5 basil leaves

DIRECTIONS

1. Clean the shrimps and peel them properly.
2. Debone the salmon and cut into small cubes. Clean oysters properly.
3. In an instant pot, add the fish stock, lemongrass, and ginger.
4. Pressure cook on high speed for 5 minutes. Add the salmon, oyster, shrimp, basil, paprika, salt, pepper, coconut milk and red chili.
5. Cook for another 5 minutes on high pressure.
6. Release the pressure and serve the soup hot.

STEAMED TILAPIA

Prep Time: 40 min   **Servings:** 2   **Kcal:** 158

INGREDIENTS

1 medium whole tilapia   1 tsp minced garlic   1 tsp oregano

1 tbsp lime juice   Salt and pepper to taste   1 tbsp shallots, chopped

1 tbsp butter   1 tsp paprika   1 tbsp tahini

1 tsp minced ginger   1 tsp thyme, minced

DIRECTIONS

1. Clean the tilapia and cut few slits on the skin.
2. In a bowl, combine the ginger, butter, lime juice, salt, paprika, pepper, thyme, oregano, shallots and tahini.
3. Mix well and marinate the fish in it for 20 minutes.
4. Wrap the fish with its juice in an aluminum foil.
5. Add a trivet in an instant pot and pour in 1 cup of water.
6. Place the fish on the trivet carefully and cover with lid.
7. Steam for 20 minutes. Serve hot.

BUTTER COD WITH ASPARAGUS

Prep Time: 10 min　　　**Servings:** 2　　　**Kcal:** 162

INGREDIENTS

2 cod fillets

1 cup asparagus, trimmed

Sea salt to taste

1 tsp paprika

1 tsp oregano

1 tbsp butter

1/2 tsp garlic powder

1 pinch sage

DIRECTIONS

1. Debone the cod fillet. Sprinkle some garlic, paprika, sage, oregano, salt, on it and coat well.
2. In an instant pot, add the butter and add the cod fillets.
3. Roast for 5 minutes and take the cod out. Add to a serving plate.
4. Add the asparagus and sprinkle some salt and paprika.
5. Sauté for 3 minutes. Add to the serving plate and serve hot.

TUNA STEAK WITH BABY POTATOES

Prep Time: 20 min   **Servings:** 2   **Kcal:** 269

INGREDIENTS

2 tuna steak	Salt to taste	Black Pepper to taste
1 tsp paprika	1 tsp garlic powder	1 tsp ginger powder
1 tbsp olive oil	1 tsp butter	1 cup baby potatoes
1 tsp mixed herbs	1 tsp thyme	½ tsp rosemary

DIRECTIONS

1. Coat the tuna steak in rosemary, thyme, paprika, salt, garlic, ginger and black pepper.
2. Let it sit for about 10 minutes.
3. Add the olive oil in the instant pot.
4. Add the tuna steak and roast for 5 minutes. Flip the tuna steaks and roast for 3 minutes.
5. Add to a serving plate.
6. Add the butter in the instant pot and add the baby potatoes.
7. Sprinkle the mixed herbs, salt, pepper and sauté for 8 minutes.
8. Serve the tuna steaks with the baby potatoes.

CRISPY SARDINE GREEN SALAD

Prep Time: 15min   **Servings:** 2   **Kcal:** 252

INGREDIENTS

- 1 cup sardines
- 1 tsp oil
- ½ tsp mixed herbs
- 10 black olives
- Salt to taste
- 1 tsp paprika
- ½ tsp onion powder
- 2 tomatoes, sliced
- Pepper to taste
- 1 tsp garlic powder
- 1 cup kale
- 2 tbsp apple cider vinegar

DIRECTIONS

1. Coat the sardines in salt, pepper, garlic, paprika, onion powder and mix well.
2. Add to the air fryer with the oil.
3. Air fry for 5 minutes. Transfer to a kitchen tissue.
4. In a mixing bowl, combine the kale, tomatoes, and black olives.
5. Add the crispy fried sardines and toss well.
6. Add the salt, pepper, mixed herbs, and apple cider vinegar.
7. Toss again and serve.

SHRIMP IN TOMATO GRAVY

Prep Time: 10 min **Servings:** 2 **Kcal:** 257

INGREDIENTS

1 ½ cup large shrimp

1 cup tomato puree

1 tsp chili flakes

Salt and pepper to taste

1 tsp mixed herbs

4 garlic cloves, sliced

1 tbsp butter

4 tbsp coconut cream

1 red jalapeno, sliced

1 tsp parsley, chopped

½ tsp cumin

DIRECTIONS

1. Peel the shrimps and clean them.
2. In an instant pot, combine the shrimp, tomato puree, chili flakes, mixed herbs, garlic, jalapeno, cumin, coconut cream, butter and parsley.
3. Cover and cook on high pressure mode for only 8 minutes.
4. Release the pressure and let it sit in the instant pot for 10 minutes.
5. Serve hot.

THE SCHEDULES

1001 DAYS OF MEAL SCHEDULES

I hope you are enjoying the recipes and that by now you are making and cooking delicious canned foods to enjoy with all your family and friends.

So you never run out of ideas and you continue cooking every day without having to worry what to cook and when, I have devised a varied and diversified 1001 day meal plan for your meals.

This way you will be able to cook for over 3 years non-stop without ever having to wonder what to choose. Just check the ingredients you need for the week, head to the grocery store and start cooking from the very first day!

Every schedule includes three meals to prepare for every day, ensuring you cook varied meals to never, ever getting tired of your canning and preserving skills. Enjoy!

WEEK 1,2	MONDAY	TUESDAY	WEDNESDAY	THURSDAY	FRIDAY	SATURDAY	SUNDAY
MEAL 1	Shredded Chicken	Sausage Balls	Potato Chicken Curry	Pesto Veggie Pasta	Chickpea Lamb Stew	Steak Bites	Pesto Veggie Pasta
MEAL 2	Chicken Hot Wings	Coated Apple Chips	Chicken Marsala	Chicken Hot Wings	Chicken Hot Wings	Minced Beef Rice	Minced Beef Rice
MEAL 3	Chicken Indian Kebab	Chocolate Muffin	Bell Pepper Lamb	Turkey Casserole	Pork Fried Rice	Chocolate Muffin	Whole Chicken Roast

WEEK 3,4	MONDAY	TUESDAY	WEDNESDAY	THURSDAY	FRIDAY	SATURDAY	SUNDAY
MEAL 1	Chicken Chimichangas	Shredded Chicken	Bell Pepper Lamb	Shredded Chicken	Cashew Nut Salad	Pesto Veggie Pasta	Shredded Chicken
MEAL 2	Tasty Chicken Wings	Coated Apple Chips	Turkey Salad	Rice Pudding	Rosemary Lamb Chops	Rosemary Lamb Chops	Turkey Skewers
MEAL 3	Whole Chicken Roast	Chocolate Muffin	Beef Curry	Turkey Casserole	Bred Sticks	Chicken Marsala	Chocolate Muffin

WEEK 5,6	MONDAY	TUESDAY	WEDNESDAY	THURSDAY	FRIDAY	SATURDAY	SUNDAY
MEAL 1	Stuffed Chicken	Crispy Pot Roast	Turkey Quiche	Turkey Quiche	Bell Pepper Lamb	Bell Pepper Lamb	Sausage Balls
MEAL 2	Coconut Curry	Tasty Chicken Wings	Pork Stew with Veggies	Steak with Cauliflower	Beef Carrot Stew	Steak with Cauliflower	Carrot Cake
MEAL 3	Herb Crusted Breast	Egg Flan	Pork Fried Rice	Chocolate Muffin	Whole Chicken Roast	Asian Lamb Chops	Chicken Marsala

WEEK 7,8	MONDAY	TUESDAY	WEDNESDAY	THURSDAY	FRIDAY	SATURDAY	SUNDAY
MEAL 1	Potato Chicken Curry	Beef Carrot Stew	Shredded Chicken	Shredded Chicken	Pesto Veggie Pasta	Fried Turkey Burgers	Potato Chicken Curry
MEAL 2	Chicken Marsala	Turkey Salad	Turkey Skewers	Turkey Stew	Pork Stew with Veggies	Chicken Marsala	Minced Beef Rice
MEAL 3	Chicken Marsala	Green Beans Pork Bites	Green Beans Pork Bites	Chicken Indian Kebab	Chicken Marsala	Crispy Chuck Roast	Asian Lamb Chops

WEEK 9,10	MONDAY	TUESDAY	WEDNESDAY	THURSDAY	FRIDAY	SATURDAY	SUNDAY
MEAL 1	Chicken Chimichangas	Potato Chicken Curry	Lamb Leg Roast	Pesto Veggie Pasta	Sausage Balls	Steak Bites	Bell Pepper Lamb
MEAL 2	Chicken Marsala	Coated Apple Chips	Coated Apple Chips	Turkey Salad	Almond Cake	Tasty Chicken Wings	Brownie
MEAL 3	Garlic Bread Pizza	Pepper Lamb Shank	Chicken Marsala	Whole Chicken Roast	Pork Fried Rice	Beef Broccoli	Beef Broccoli

WEEK 11,12	MONDAY	TUESDAY	WEDNESDAY	THURSDAY	FRIDAY	SATURDAY	SUNDAY
MEAL 1	Sausage Balls	Chicken Chimichangas	Potato Chicken Curry	Steak Bites	Steak Bites	Crispy Pot Roast	Honey Lamb Chops
MEAL 2	Pork Chops	Almond Cake	Chicken Hot Wings	Rice Pudding	Coconut Curry	Turkey Salad	Carrot Cake
MEAL 3	Pork Fried Rice	Pork Fried Rice	Green Beans Pork Bites	Asian Lamb Chops	Green Beans Pork Bites	Beef Curry	Garlic Bread Pizza

WEEK 13,14	MONDAY	TUESDAY	WEDNESDAY	THURSDAY	FRIDAY	SATURDAY	SUNDAY
MEAL 1	Stuffed Chicken	Spinach Turkey Breasts	Crispy Pot Roast	Turkey Quiche	Fried Turkey Burgers	Steak Bites	Fried chicken
MEAL 2	Pork Stew with Veggies	Citrus Turkey Roast	Pork Stew with Veggies	Carrot Cake	Turkey Skewers	Coconut Curry	Turkey Skewers
MEAL 3	Pork Broccoli Stir Fry	Pork Fried Rice	Whole Chicken Roast	Chicken Indian Kebab	Egg Flan	Beef Curry	Beef Curry

WEEK 15,16	MONDAY	TUESDAY	WEDNESDAY	THURSDAY	FRIDAY	SATURDAY	SUNDAY
MEAL 1	Cashew Nut Salad	Beef Carrot Stew	Bell Pepper Lamb	Chickpea Lamb Stew	Potato Chicken Curry	Honey Lamb Chops	Beef Carrot Stew
MEAL 2	Steak with Cauliflower	Beef Carrot Stew	Carrot Cake	Almond Cake	Brownie	Rice Pudding	Chicken Marsala
MEAL 3	Pork Broccoli Stir Fry	Turkey Casserole	Asian Lamb Chops	Beef Curry	Green Beans Pork Bites	Turkey Casserole	Whole Chicken Roast

WEEK 17,18	MONDAY	TUESDAY	WEDNESDAY	THURSDAY	FRIDAY	SATURDAY	SUNDAY
MEAL 1	Stuffed Chicken	Chicken Chimichangas	Shredded Chicken	Steak Bites	Cashew Nut Salad	Spinach Turkey Breasts	Pesto Veggie Pasta
MEAL 2	Pork Stew with Veggies	Pork Chops	Coated Apple Chips	Chicken Marsala	Citrus Turkey Roast	Chicken Hot Wings	Tasty Chicken Wings
MEAL 3	Green Beans Pork Bites	Asian Lamb Chops	Bell Pepper Lamb	Beef Broccoli	Bred Sticks	Herb Crusted Breast	Asian Lamb Chops

WEEK 19,20	MONDAY	TUESDAY	WEDNESDAY	THURSDAY	FRIDAY	SATURDAY	SUNDAY
MEAL 1	Fried Turkey Burgers	Crispy Turkey Strips	Fried Turkey Burgers	Cashew Nut Salad	Honey Lamb Chops	Turkey Quiche	Honey Lamb Chops
MEAL 2	Turkey Skewers	Pork Stew with Veggies	Coated Apple Chips	Turkey Skewers	Ribeye Fried Steak	Ribeye Fried Steak	Turkey Skewers
MEAL 3	Turkey Balls	Turkey Casserole	Egg Flan	Beef Broccoli	Chicken Marsala	Green Beans Pork Bites	Chicken Indian Kebab

WEEK 21,22	MONDAY	TUESDAY	WEDNESDAY	THURSDAY	FRIDAY	SATURDAY	SUNDAY
MEAL 1	Chicken Chimichangas	Steak Bites	Turkey Quiche	Fried Turkey Burgers	Lamb Leg Roast	Potato Chicken Curry	Potato Chicken Curry
MEAL 2	Turkey Salad	Pork Chops	Beef Carrot Stew	Brownie	Chicken Hot Wings	Almond Cake	Rice Pudding
MEAL 3	Chicken Indian Kebab	Pork Broccoli Stir Fry	Garlic Bread Pizza	Chicken Marsala	Beef Curry	Turkey Balls	Bred Sticks

WEEK 23,24	MONDAY	TUESDAY	WEDNESDAY	THURSDAY	FRIDAY	SATURDAY	SUNDAY
MEAL 1	Crispy Turkey Strips	Crispy Turkey Strips	Fried chicken	Stuffed Chicken	Turkey Quiche	Stuffed Chicken	Spinach Turkey Breasts
MEAL 2	Turkey Stew	Turkey Skewers	Pork Chops	Citrus Turkey Roast	Carrot Cake	Almond Cake	Citrus Turkey Roast
MEAL 3	Turkey Casserole	Chicken Marsala	Pork Broccoli Stir Fry	Chicken Marsala	Pork Fried Rice	Garlic Bread Pizza	Turkey Balls

WEEK 25,26	MONDAY	TUESDAY	WEDNESDAY	THURSDAY	FRIDAY	SATURDAY	SUNDAY
MEAL 1	Turkey Quiche	Potato Chicken Curry	Lamb Skewers	Cashew Nut Salad	Shredded Chicken	Crispy Pot Roast	Spinach Turkey Breasts
MEAL 2	Citrus Turkey Roast	Chicken Hot Wings	Chicken Marsala	Coated Apple Chips	Turkey Salad	Coated Apple Chips	Ribeye Fried Steak
MEAL 3	Turkey Casserole	Whole Chicken Roast	Bell Pepper Lamb	Whole Chicken Roast	Pork Broccoli Stir Fry	Pepper Lamb Shank	Egg Flan

WEEK 27,28	MONDAY	TUESDAY	WEDNESDAY	THURSDAY	FRIDAY	SATURDAY	SUNDAY
MEAL 1	Spinach Turkey Breasts	Chickpea Lamb Stew	Turkey Quiche	Fried chicken	Steak Bites	Cashew Nut Salad	Fried Turkey Burgers
MEAL 2	Steak with Cauliflower	Citrus Turkey Roast	Rosemary Lamb Chops	Turkey Stew	Pork Chops	Minced Beef Rice	Pork Stew with Veggies
MEAL 3	Crispy Chuck Roast	Chicken Marsala	Pork Broccoli Stir Fry	Pork Fried Rice	Pork Fried Rice	Pepper Lamb Shank	Chicken Indian Kebab

WEEK 29,30	MONDAY	TUESDAY	WEDNESDAY	THURSDAY	FRIDAY	SATURDAY	SUNDAY
MEAL 1	Shredded Chicken	Steak Bites	Potato Chicken Curry	Spinach Turkey Breasts	Turkey Quiche	Stuffed Chicken	Crispy Pot Roast
MEAL 2	Citrus Turkey Roast	Coated Apple Chips	Pork Chops	Beef Carrot Stew	Pork Stew with Veggies	Turkey Skewers	Ribeye Fried Steak
MEAL 3	Whole Chicken Roast	Crispy Chuck Roast	Beef Meatballs	Garlic Bread Pizza	Crispy Chuck Roast	Pork Broccoli Stir Fry	Pepper Lamb Shank

WEEK 31,32	MONDAY	TUESDAY	WEDNESDAY	THURSDAY	FRIDAY	SATURDAY	SUNDAY
MEAL 1	Crispy Pot Roast	Fried Turkey Burgers	Pesto Veggie Pasta	Potato Chicken Curry	Steak Bites	Shredded Chicken	Steak Bites
MEAL 2	Ribeye Fried Steak	Pork Stew with Veggies	Turkey Salad	Brownie	Turkey Skewers	Pork Chops	Turkey Stew
MEAL 3	Pork Broccoli Stir Fry	Turkey Balls	Beef Curry	Whole Chicken Roast	Turkey Balls	Chicken Marsala	Pork Broccoli Stir Fry

WEEK 33,34	MONDAY	TUESDAY	WEDNESDAY	THURSDAY	FRIDAY	SATURDAY	SUNDAY
MEAL 1	Steak Bites	Crispy Turkey Strips	Pesto Veggie Pasta	Honey Lamb Chops	Stuffed Chicken	Stuffed Chicken	Turkey Quiche
MEAL 2	Turkey Skewers	Turkey Skewers	Turkey Skewers	Coconut Curry	Pork Stew with Veggies	Tasty Chicken Wings	Brownie
MEAL 3	Beef Broccoli	Herb Crusted Breast	Whole Chicken Roast	Chocolate Muffin	Whole Chicken Roast	Chicken Marsala	Pork Fried Rice

WEEK 35,36	MONDAY	TUESDAY	WEDNESDAY	THURSDAY	FRIDAY	SATURDAY	SUNDAY
MEAL 1	Turkey Quiche	Lamb Skewers	Potato Chicken Curry	Crispy Pot Roast	Shredded Chicken	Beef Carrot Stew	Lamb Skewers
MEAL 2	Minced Beef Rice	Chicken Marsala	Citrus Turkey Roast	Steak with Cauliflower	Citrus Turkey Roast	Ribeye Fried Steak	Chicken Hot Wings
MEAL 3	Beef Curry	Garlic Bread Pizza	Beef Broccoli	Pork Broccoli Stir Fry	Crispy Chuck Roast	Whole Chicken Roast	Chicken Marsala

WEEK 37,38	MONDAY	TUESDAY	WEDNESDAY	THURSDAY	FRIDAY	SATURDAY	SUNDAY
MEAL 1	Chicken Chimichangas	Potato Chicken Curry	Honey Lamb Chops	Chicken Chimichangas	Bell Pepper Lamb	Pesto Veggie Pasta	Crispy Turkey Strips
MEAL 2	Turkey Salad	Beef Carrot Stew	Turkey Stew	Pork Stew with Veggies	Minced Beef Rice	Pork Chops	Minced Beef Rice
MEAL 3	Garlic Bread Pizza	Beef Broccoli	Bred Sticks	Pork Fried Rice	Chocolate Muffin	Green Beans Pork Bites	Pepper Lamb Shank

WEEK 39,40	MONDAY	TUESDAY	WEDNESDAY	THURSDAY	FRIDAY	SATURDAY	SUNDAY
MEAL 1	Sausage Balls	Fried chicken	Crispy Turkey Strips	Chickpea Lamb Stew	Potato Chicken Curry	Chickpea Lamb Stew	Chickpea Lamb Stew
MEAL 2	Turkey Stew	Pork Stew with Veggies	Citrus Turkey Roast	Brownie	Turkey Stew	Ribeye Fried Steak	Steak with Cauliflower
MEAL 3	Beef Meatballs	Asian Lamb Chops	Bell Pepper Lamb	Green Beans Pork Bites	Herb Crusted Breast	Whole Chicken Roast	Pepper Lamb Shank

41,42	MONDAY	TUESDAY	WEDNESDAY	THURSDAY	FRIDAY	SATURDAY	SUNDAY
MEAL 1	Potato Chicken Curry	Beef Carrot Stew	Chicken Chimichangas	Sausage Balls	Pesto Veggie Pasta	Steak Bites	Stuffed Chicken
MEAL 2	Ribeye Fried Steak	Chicken Marsala	Steak with Cauliflower	Steak with Cauliflower	Carrot Cake	Steak with Cauliflower	Rosemary Lamb Chops
MEAL 3	Turkey Balls	Chicken Indian Kebab	Turkey Balls	Beef Broccoli	Pork Broccoli Stir Fry	Pepper Lamb Shank	Chicken Marsala

43,44	MONDAY	TUESDAY	WEDNESDAY	THURSDAY	FRIDAY	SATURDAY	SUNDAY
MEAL 1	Fried chicken	Sausage Balls	Pesto Veggie Pasta	Lamb Skewers	Beef Carrot Stew	Sausage Balls	Turkey Quiche
MEAL 2	Minced Beef Rice	Steak with Cauliflower	Citrus Turkey Roast	Brownie	Coated Apple Chips	Minced Beef Rice	Turkey Skewers
MEAL 3	Herb Crusted Breast	Bred Sticks	Asian Lamb Chops	Garlic Bread Pizza	Bell Pepper Lamb	Bell Pepper Lamb	Bred Sticks

45,46	MONDAY	TUESDAY	WEDNESDAY	THURSDAY	FRIDAY	SATURDAY	SUNDAY
MEAL 1	Beef Carrot Stew	Lamb Leg Roast	Crispy Pot Roast	Steak Bites	Sausage Balls	Crispy Turkey Strips	Cashew Nut Salad
MEAL 2	Beef Carrot Stew	Coated Apple Chips	Rosemary Lamb Chops	Chicken Marsala	Pork Stew with Veggies	Coconut Curry	Minced Beef Rice
MEAL 3	Asian Lamb Chops	Garlic Bread Pizza	Bred Sticks	Beef Curry	Chicken Indian Kebab	Asian Lamb Chops	Pork Broccoli Stir Fry

47,48	MONDAY	TUESDAY	WEDNESDAY	THURSDAY	FRIDAY	SATURDAY	SUNDAY
MEAL 1	Shredded Chicken	Bell Pepper Lamb	Chickpea Lamb Stew	Lamb Leg Roast	Chickpea Lamb Stew	Stuffed Chicken	Bell Pepper Lamb
MEAL 2	Beef Carrot Stew	Chicken Marsala	Beef Carrot Stew	Rosemary Lamb Chops	Rice Pudding	Coconut Curry	Turkey Skewers
MEAL 3	Turkey Balls	Green Beans Pork Bites	Green Beans Pork Bites	Bred Sticks	Chicken Marsala	Turkey Casserole	Beef Broccoli

49,50	MONDAY	TUESDAY	WEDNESDAY	THURSDAY	FRIDAY	SATURDAY	SUNDAY
MEAL 1	Crispy Pot Roast	Potato Chicken Curry	Sausage Balls	Fried Turkey Burgers	Chicken Chimichangas	Pesto Veggie Pasta	Crispy Turkey Strips
MEAL 2	Ribeye Fried Steak	Chicken Hot Wings	Carrot Cake	Chicken Hot Wings	Brownie	Chicken Marsala	Chicken Hot Wings
MEAL 3	Herb Crusted Breast	Turkey Balls	Pork Fried Rice	Beef Curry	Chocolate Muffin	Chicken Indian Kebab	Chicken Indian Kebab

51,52	MONDAY	TUESDAY	WEDNESDAY	THURSDAY	FRIDAY	SATURDAY	SUNDAY
MEAL 1	Lamb Skewers	Potato Chicken Curry	Lamb Skewers	Bell Pepper Lamb	Pesto Veggie Pasta	Potato Chicken Curry	Turkey Quiche
MEAL 2	Rosemary Lamb Chops	Brownie	Citrus Turkey Roast	Citrus Turkey Roast	Citrus Turkey Roast	Ribeye Fried Steak	Rosemary Lamb Chops
MEAL 3	Beef Broccoli	Whole Chicken Roast	Chocolate Muffin	Beef Meatballs	Turkey Balls	Egg Flan	Beef Meatballs

53,54	MONDAY	TUESDAY	WEDNESDAY	THURSDAY	FRIDAY	SATURDAY	SUNDAY
MEAL 1	Honey Lamb Chops	Crispy Turkey Strips	Turkey Quiche	Chickpea Lamb Stew	Sausage Balls	Spinach Turkey Breasts	Lamb Leg Roast
MEAL 2	Rosemary Lamb Chops	Coated Apple Chips	Pork Chops	Brownie	Rice Pudding	Turkey Skewers	Almond Cake
MEAL 3	Green Beans Pork Bites	Asian Lamb Chops	Herb Crusted Breast	Pork Fried Rice	Asian Lamb Chops	Turkey Casserole	Asian Lamb Chops

55,56	MONDAY	TUESDAY	WEDNESDAY	THURSDAY	FRIDAY	SATURDAY	SUNDAY
MEAL 1	Stuffed Chicken	Crispy Turkey Strips	Sausage Balls	Cashew Nut Salad	Stuffed Chicken	Pesto Veggie Pasta	Cashew Nut Salad
MEAL 2	Minced Beef Rice	Beef Carrot Stew	Coconut Curry	Carrot Cake	Citrus Turkey Roast	Chicken Marsala	Turkey Stew
MEAL 3	Chicken Marsala	Chicken Indian Kebab	Pork Broccoli Stir Fry	Whole Chicken Roast	Whole Chicken Roast	Garlic Bread Pizza	Beef Curry

57, 58	MONDAY	TUESDAY	WEDNESDAY	THURSDAY	FRIDAY	SATURDAY	SUNDAY
MEAL 1	Cashew Nut Salad	Chickpea Lamb Stew	Crispy Turkey Strips	Steak Bites	Pesto Veggie Pasta	Crispy Pot Roast	Honey Lamb Chops
MEAL 2	Tasty Chicken Wings	Turkey Skewers	Pork Stew with Veggies	Coated Apple Chips	Ribeye Fried Steak	Chicken Marsala	Rice Pudding
MEAL 3	Bell Pepper Lamb	Chicken Indian Kebab	Bred Sticks	Egg Flan	Turkey Balls	Chicken Indian Kebab	Chocolate Muffin

59, 60	MONDAY	TUESDAY	WEDNESDAY	THURSDAY	FRIDAY	SATURDAY	SUNDAY
MEAL 1	Chickpea Lamb Stew	Potato Chicken Curry	Spinach Turkey Breasts	Sausage Balls	Lamb Skewers	Steak Bites	Fried Turkey Burgers
MEAL 2	Rosemary Lamb Chops	Beef Carrot Stew	Beef Carrot Stew	Ribeye Fried Steak	Almond Cake	Turkey Skewers	Chicken Hot Wings
MEAL 3	Pork Broccoli Stir Fry	Chicken Marsala	Pork Fried Rice	Crispy Chuck Roast	Chicken Indian Kebab	Whole Chicken Roast	Turkey Balls

61, 62	MONDAY	TUESDAY	WEDNESDAY	THURSDAY	FRIDAY	SATURDAY	SUNDAY
MEAL 1	Honey Lamb Chops	Beef Carrot Stew	Turkey Quiche	Cashew Nut Salad	Spinach Turkey Breasts	Honey Lamb Chops	Honey Lamb Chops
MEAL 2	Coconut Curry	Rice Pudding	Pork Stew with Veggies	Carrot Cake	Minced Beef Rice	Carrot Cake	Turkey Salad
MEAL 3	Beef Broccoli	Crispy Chuck Roast	Bell Pepper Lamb	Beef Meatballs	Turkey Balls	Egg Flan	Beef Meatballs

63, 64	MONDAY	TUESDAY	WEDNESDAY	THURSDAY	FRIDAY	SATURDAY	SUNDAY
MEAL 1	Lamb Skewers	Pesto Veggie Pasta	Lamb Leg Roast	Chicken Chimichangas	Spinach Turkey Breasts	Bell Pepper Lamb	Turkey Quiche
MEAL 2	Citrus Turkey Roast	Almond Cake	Rice Pudding	Chicken Marsala	Carrot Cake	Turkey Stew	Coated Apple Chips
MEAL 3	Pepper Lamb Shank	Beef Broccoli	Turkey Balls	Turkey Casserole	Turkey Balls	Pork Fried Rice	Bell Pepper Lamb

65,66	MONDAY	TUESDAY	WEDNESDAY	THURSDAY	FRIDAY	SATURDAY	SUNDAY
MEAL 1	Fried chicken	Chicken Chimichangas	Crispy Pot Roast	Turkey Quiche	Fried Turkey Burgers	Lamb Skewers	Spinach Turkey Breasts
MEAL 2	Turkey Salad	Beef Carrot Stew	Turkey Skewers	Turkey Stew	Turkey Salad	Chicken Marsala	Chicken Hot Wings
MEAL 3	Green Beans Pork Bites	Bell Pepper Lamb	Garlic Bread Pizza	Whole Chicken Roast	Chicken Indian Kebab	Green Beans Pork Bites	Garlic Bread Pizza

67,68	MONDAY	TUESDAY	WEDNESDAY	THURSDAY	FRIDAY	SATURDAY	SUNDAY
MEAL 1	Honey Lamb Chops	Sausage Balls	Potato Chicken Curry	Lamb Leg Roast	Fried Turkey Burgers	Honey Lamb Chops	Pesto Veggie Pasta
MEAL 2	Turkey Salad	Rice Pudding	Ribeye Fried Steak	Almond Cake	Pork Stew with Veggies	Rosemary Lamb Chops	Almond Cake
MEAL 3	Crispy Chuck Roast	Pepper Lamb Shank	Herb Crusted Breast	Pork Fried Rice	Pork Broccoli Stir Fry	Chicken Marsala	Pepper Lamb Shank

69,70	MONDAY	TUESDAY	WEDNESDAY	THURSDAY	FRIDAY	SATURDAY	SUNDAY
MEAL 1	Stuffed Chicken	Shredded Chicken	Stuffed Chicken	Shredded Chicken	Beef Carrot Stew	Potato Chicken Curry	Turkey Quiche
MEAL 2	Ribeye Fried Steak	Turkey Stew	Brownie	Chicken Hot Wings	Tasty Chicken Wings	Pork Stew with Veggies	Turkey Salad
MEAL 3	Beef Broccoli	Egg Flan	Bred Sticks	Chocolate Muffin	Asian Lamb Chops	Garlic Bread Pizza	Bred Sticks

71,72	MONDAY	TUESDAY	WEDNESDAY	THURSDAY	FRIDAY	SATURDAY	SUNDAY
MEAL 1	Lamb Leg Roast	Lamb Skewers	Stuffed Chicken	Stuffed Chicken	Crispy Pot Roast	Steak Bites	Spinach Turkey Breasts
MEAL 2	Turkey Stew	Steak with Cauliflower	Rosemary Lamb Chops	Rosemary Lamb Chops	Brownie	Turkey Skewers	Pork Stew with Veggies
MEAL 3	Garlic Bread Pizza	Turkey Casserole	Turkey Casserole	Chicken Marsala	Pork Fried Rice	Egg Flan	Turkey Casserole

73,74	MONDAY	TUESDAY	WEDNESDAY	THURSDAY	FRIDAY	SATURDAY	SUNDAY
MEAL 1	Cashew Nut Salad	Bell Pepper Lamb	Pesto Veggie Pasta	Stuffed Chicken	Crispy Pot Roast	Cashew Nut Salad	Crispy Turkey Strips
MEAL 2	Coated Apple Chips	Carrot Cake	Ribeye Fried Steak	Turkey Salad	Steak with Cauliflower	Steak with Cauliflower	Carrot Cake
MEAL 3	Beef Curry	Turkey Balls	Chicken Marsala	Egg Flan	Beef Broccoli	Pepper Lamb Shank	Whole Chicken Roast

75,76	MONDAY	TUESDAY	WEDNESDAY	THURSDAY	FRIDAY	SATURDAY	SUNDAY
MEAL 1	Fried Turkey Burgers	Stuffed Chicken	Honey Lamb Chops	Bell Pepper Lamb	Turkey Quiche	Cashew Nut Salad	Lamb Skewers
MEAL 2	Coated Apple Chips	Chicken Hot Wings	Brownie	Rosemary Lamb Chops	Brownie	Coconut Curry	Turkey Skewers
MEAL 3	Pepper Lamb Shank	Bred Sticks	Chocolate Muffin	Asian Lamb Chops	Bred Sticks	Chocolate Muffin	Pepper Lamb Shank

77,78	MONDAY	TUESDAY	WEDNESDAY	THURSDAY	FRIDAY	SATURDAY	SUNDAY
MEAL 1	Spinach Turkey Breasts	Lamb Skewers	Potato Chicken Curry	Lamb Skewers	Lamb Leg Roast	Chickpea Lamb Stew	Stuffed Chicken
MEAL 2	Ribeye Fried Steak	Coconut Curry	Minced Beef Rice	Steak with Cauliflower	Turkey Skewers	Turkey Stew	Coated Apple Chips
MEAL 3	Garlic Bread Pizza	Beef Curry	Chicken Indian Kebab	Turkey Casserole	Crispy Chuck Roast	Crispy Chuck Roast	Bred Sticks

79,80	MONDAY	TUESDAY	WEDNESDAY	THURSDAY	FRIDAY	SATURDAY	SUNDAY
MEAL 1	Lamb Skewers	Potato Chicken Curry	Crispy Turkey Strips	Cashew Nut Salad	Fried Turkey Burgers	Lamb Leg Roast	Pesto Veggie Pasta
MEAL 2	Minced Beef Rice	Pork Chops	Beef Carrot Stew	Minced Beef Rice	Chicken Marsala	Pork Chops	Chicken Marsala
MEAL 3	Green Beans Pork Bites	Chicken Marsala	Chicken Indian Kebab	Whole Chicken Roast	Beef Curry	Chicken Indian Kebab	Bred Sticks

81,82	MONDAY	TUESDAY	WEDNESDAY	THURSDAY	FRIDAY	SATURDAY	SUNDAY
MEAL 1	Chicken Chimichangas	Honey Lamb Chops	Turkey Quiche	Turkey Quiche	Shredded Chicken	Shredded Chicken	Lamb Skewers
MEAL 2	Citrus Turkey Roast	Rosemary Lamb Chops	Citrus Turkey Roast	Pork Stew with Veggies	Steak with Cauliflower	Chicken Marsala	Chicken Marsala
MEAL 3	Garlic Bread Pizza	Pork Fried Rice	Pork Fried Rice	Bred Sticks	Bred Sticks	Pork Broccoli Stir Fry	Bell Pepper Lamb

83,84	MONDAY	TUESDAY	WEDNESDAY	THURSDAY	FRIDAY	SATURDAY	SUNDAY
MEAL 1	Lamb Skewers	Lamb Leg Roast	Potato Chicken Curry	Cashew Nut Salad	Lamb Leg Roast	Chicken Chimichangas	Potato Chicken Curry
MEAL 2	Tasty Chicken Wings	Tasty Chicken Wings	Carrot Cake	Turkey Salad	Carrot Cake	Turkey Salad	Steak with Cauliflower
MEAL 3	Bred Sticks	Pepper Lamb Shank	Whole Chicken Roast	Chicken Marsala	Green Beans Pork Bites	Beef Meatballs	Pork Broccoli Stir Fry

85,86	MONDAY	TUESDAY	WEDNESDAY	THURSDAY	FRIDAY	SATURDAY	SUNDAY
MEAL 1	Steak Bites	Bell Pepper Lamb	Sausage Balls	Bell Pepper Lamb	Sausage Balls	Fried chicken	Lamb Leg Roast
MEAL 2	Turkey Salad	Citrus Turkey Roast	Steak with Cauliflower	Turkey Skewers	Rice Pudding	Turkey Stew	Turkey Stew
MEAL 3	Garlic Bread Pizza	Pepper Lamb Shank	Turkey Casserole	Bell Pepper Lamb	Pepper Lamb Shank	Turkey Balls	Egg Flan

87,88	MONDAY	TUESDAY	WEDNESDAY	THURSDAY	FRIDAY	SATURDAY	SUNDAY
MEAL 1	Shredded Chicken	Pesto Veggie Pasta	Crispy Pot Roast	Potato Chicken Curry	Turkey Quiche	Shredded Chicken	Fried chicken
MEAL 2	Beef Carrot Stew	Carrot Cake	Pork Stew with Veggies	Almond Cake	Rosemary Lamb Chops	Turkey Salad	Coated Apple Chips
MEAL 3	Green Beans Pork Bites	Whole Chicken Roast	Chicken Indian Kebab	Pepper Lamb Shank	Chicken Indian Kebab	Turkey Casserole	Pork Broccoli Stir Fry

89,90	MONDAY	TUESDAY	WEDNESDAY	THURSDAY	FRIDAY	SATURDAY	SUNDAY
MEAL 1	Steak Bites	Lamb Leg Roast	Shredded Chicken	Lamb Leg Roast	Chicken Chimichangas	Potato Chicken Curry	Pesto Veggie Pasta
MEAL 2	Turkey Stew	Citrus Turkey Roast	Almond Cake	Coated Apple Chips	Citrus Turkey Roast	Coated Apple Chips	Turkey Stew
MEAL 3	Turkey Balls	Green Beans Pork Bites	Pork Fried Rice	Pork Broccoli Stir Fry	Green Beans Pork Bites	Herb Crusted Breast	Pork Fried Rice

91,92	MONDAY	TUESDAY	WEDNESDAY	THURSDAY	FRIDAY	SATURDAY	SUNDAY
MEAL 1	Beef Carrot Stew	Fried Turkey Burgers	Lamb Leg Roast	Lamb Leg Roast	Stuffed Chicken	Steak Bites	Shredded Chicken
MEAL 2	Coconut Curry	Ribeye Fried Steak	Chicken Hot Wings	Almond Cake	Pork Stew with Veggies	Tasty Chicken Wings	Carrot Cake
MEAL 3	Beef Meatballs	Whole Chicken Roast	Beef Broccoli	Egg Flan	Turkey Casserole	Whole Chicken Roast	Garlic Bread Pizza

93,94	MONDAY	TUESDAY	WEDNESDAY	THURSDAY	FRIDAY	SATURDAY	SUNDAY
MEAL 1	Fried chicken	Spinach Turkey Breasts	Honey Lamb Chops	Stuffed Chicken	Stuffed Chicken	Cashew Nut Salad	Chicken Chimichangas
MEAL 2	Pork Chops	Chicken Marsala	Tasty Chicken Wings	Citrus Turkey Roast	Steak with Cauliflower	Ribeye Fried Steak	Carrot Cake
MEAL 3	Egg Flan	Bell Pepper Lamb	Pork Broccoli Stir Fry	Herb Crusted Breast	Egg Flan	Beef Curry	Pork Fried Rice

95,96	MONDAY	TUESDAY	WEDNESDAY	THURSDAY	FRIDAY	SATURDAY	SUNDAY
MEAL 1	Sausage Balls	Crispy Turkey Strips	Fried Turkey Burgers	Crispy Turkey Strips	Shredded Chicken	Potato Chicken Curry	Crispy Turkey Strips
MEAL 2	Steak with Cauliflower	Turkey Stew	Ribeye Fried Steak	Almond Cake	Carrot Cake	Brownie	Minced Beef Rice
MEAL 3	Chocolate Muffin	Chicken Marsala	Pork Broccoli Stir Fry	Crispy Chuck Roast	Beef Broccoli	Egg Flan	Pork Fried Rice

97,98	MONDAY	TUESDAY	WEDNESDAY	THURSDAY	FRIDAY	SATURDAY	SUNDAY
MEAL 1	Fried Turkey Burgers	Stuffed Chicken	Cashew Nut Salad	Chickpea Lamb Stew	Sausage Balls	Bell Pepper Lamb	Shredded Chicken
MEAL 2	Rice Pudding	Carrot Cake	Chicken Hot Wings	Coconut Curry	Turkey Skewers	Steak with Cauliflower	Citrus Turkey Roast
MEAL 3	Beef Meatballs	Whole Chicken Roast	Pork Broccoli Stir Fry	Chocolate Muffin	Beef Curry	Pepper Lamb Shank	Green Beans Pork Bites

99,100	MONDAY	TUESDAY	WEDNESDAY	THURSDAY	FRIDAY	SATURDAY	SUNDAY
MEAL 1	Fried Turkey Burgers	Lamb Leg Roast	Steak Bites	Shredded Chicken	Pesto Veggie Pasta	Stuffed Chicken	Turkey Quiche
MEAL 2	Turkey Salad	Turkey Skewers	Citrus Turkey Roast	Rosemary Lamb Chops	Brownie	Pork Chops	Pork Stew with Veggies
MEAL 3	Bred Sticks	Chicken Marsala	Garlic Bread Pizza	Green Beans Pork Bites	Chocolate Muffin	Bell Pepper Lamb	Turkey Balls

101,102	MONDAY	TUESDAY	WEDNESDAY	THURSDAY	FRIDAY	SATURDAY	SUNDAY
MEAL 1	Shredded Chicken	Crispy Turkey Strips	Pesto Veggie Pasta	Beef Carrot Stew	Lamb Leg Roast	Chickpea Lamb Stew	Turkey Quiche
MEAL 2	Coated Apple Chips	Turkey Skewers	Coconut Curry	Turkey Salad	Citrus Turkey Roast	Rosemary Lamb Chops	Turkey Skewers
MEAL 3	Asian Lamb Chops	Beef Meatballs	Chocolate Muffin	Egg Flan	Beef Curry	Bell Pepper Lamb	Turkey Balls

103,104	MONDAY	TUESDAY	WEDNESDAY	THURSDAY	FRIDAY	SATURDAY	SUNDAY
MEAL 1	Fried Turkey Burgers	Beef Carrot Stew	Potato Chicken Curry	Crispy Turkey Strips	Lamb Leg Roast	Pesto Veggie Pasta	Honey Lamb Chops
MEAL 2	Rosemary Lamb Chops	Brownie	Chicken Marsala	Rice Pudding	Steak with Cauliflower	Citrus Turkey Roast	Pork Stew with Veggies
MEAL 3	Egg Flan	Bred Sticks	Green Beans Pork Bites	Pepper Lamb Shank	Green Beans Pork Bites	Chicken Indian Kebab	Chicken Marsala

105,106	MONDAY	TUESDAY	WEDNESDAY	THURSDAY	FRIDAY	SATURDAY	SUNDAY
MEAL 1	Cashew Nut Salad	Spinach Turkey Breasts	Steak Bites	Chickpea Lamb Stew	Sausage Balls	Turkey Quiche	Lamb Leg Roast
MEAL 2	Coconut Curry	Minced Beef Rice	Turkey Salad	Coconut Curry	Coconut Curry	Steak with Cauliflower	Rosemary Lamb Chops
MEAL 3	Pork Broccoli Stir Fry	Pork Fried Rice	Pork Broccoli Stir Fry	Herb Crusted Breast	Beef Curry	Green Beans Pork Bites	Crispy Chuck Roast

107,108	MONDAY	TUESDAY	WEDNESDAY	THURSDAY	FRIDAY	SATURDAY	SUNDAY
MEAL 1	Pesto Veggie Pasta	Crispy Pot Roast	Lamb Leg Roast	Beef Carrot Stew	Pesto Veggie Pasta	Lamb Skewers	Stuffed Chicken
MEAL 2	Pork Stew with Veggies	Chicken Hot Wings	Turkey Salad	Turkey Skewers	Ribeye Fried Steak	Coconut Curry	Citrus Turkey Roast
MEAL 3	Pork Broccoli Stir Fry	Pork Broccoli Stir Fry	Garlic Bread Pizza	Chicken Indian Kebab	Chocolate Muffin	Whole Chicken Roast	Chicken Indian Kebab

109,110	MONDAY	TUESDAY	WEDNESDAY	THURSDAY	FRIDAY	SATURDAY	SUNDAY
MEAL 1	Lamb Leg Roast	Fried chicken	Cashew Nut Salad	Pesto Veggie Pasta	Chickpea Lamb Stew	Lamb Skewers	Turkey Quiche
MEAL 2	Pork Stew with Veggies	Pork Chops	Pork Stew with Veggies	Turkey Skewers	Rice Pudding	Turkey Skewers	Pork Chops
MEAL 3	Bred Sticks	Pepper Lamb Shank	Chicken Indian Kebab	Chocolate Muffin	Pork Fried Rice	Pork Fried Rice	Herb Crusted Breast

111,112	MONDAY	TUESDAY	WEDNESDAY	THURSDAY	FRIDAY	SATURDAY	SUNDAY
MEAL 1	Cashew Nut Salad	Fried chicken	Lamb Skewers	Lamb Skewers	Fried Turkey Burgers	Lamb Leg Roast	Beef Carrot Stew
MEAL 2	Turkey Salad	Chicken Marsala	Steak with Cauliflower	Chicken Marsala	Citrus Turkey Roast	Almond Cake	Almond Cake
MEAL 3	Whole Chicken Roast	Green Beans Pork Bites	Bred Sticks	Beef Curry	Beef Curry	Pork Broccoli Stir Fry	Beef Meatballs

113,114	MONDAY	TUESDAY	WEDNESDAY	THURSDAY	FRIDAY	SATURDAY	SUNDAY
MEAL 1	Crispy Pot Roast	Potato Chicken Curry	Fried chicken	Lamb Leg Roast	Lamb Skewers	Pesto Veggie Pasta	Chickpea Lamb Stew
MEAL 2	Pork Stew with Veggies	Almond Cake	Turkey Salad	Citrus Turkey Roast	Turkey Stew	Minced Beef Rice	Citrus Turkey Roast
MEAL 3	Beef Meatballs	Chocolate Muffin	Crispy Chuck Roast	Chocolate Muffin	Pepper Lamb Shank	Crispy Chuck Roast	Turkey Casserole

115,116	MONDAY	TUESDAY	WEDNESDAY	THURSDAY	FRIDAY	SATURDAY	SUNDAY
MEAL 1	Crispy Pot Roast	Bell Pepper Lamb	Stuffed Chicken	Fried chicken	Potato Chicken Curry	Cashew Nut Salad	Crispy Turkey Strips
MEAL 2	Ribeye Fried Steak	Chicken Hot Wings	Brownie	Turkey Skewers	Chicken Marsala	Carrot Cake	Beef Carrot Stew
MEAL 3	Herb Crusted Breast	Green Beans Pork Bites	Pepper Lamb Shank	Bell Pepper Lamb	Crispy Chuck Roast	Bred Sticks	Egg Flan

117,118	MONDAY	TUESDAY	WEDNESDAY	THURSDAY	FRIDAY	SATURDAY	SUNDAY
MEAL 1	Crispy Turkey Strips	Pesto Veggie Pasta	Fried chicken	Bell Pepper Lamb	Bell Pepper Lamb	Bell Pepper Lamb	Chickpea Lamb Stew
MEAL 2	Ribeye Fried Steak	Tasty Chicken Wings	Turkey Skewers	Carrot Cake	Tasty Chicken Wings	Turkey Skewers	Citrus Turkey Roast
MEAL 3	Chocolate Muffin	Beef Curry	Crispy Chuck Roast	Turkey Balls	Herb Crusted Breast	Beef Meatballs	Chicken Indian Kebab

119,120	MONDAY	TUESDAY	WEDNESDAY	THURSDAY	FRIDAY	SATURDAY	SUNDAY
MEAL 1	Steak Bites	Sausage Balls	Beef Carrot Stew	Crispy Pot Roast	Crispy Pot Roast	Chickpea Lamb Stew	Bell Pepper Lamb
MEAL 2	Ribeye Fried Steak	Beef Carrot Stew	Coconut Curry	Coated Apple Chips	Coated Apple Chips	Turkey Salad	Chicken Hot Wings
MEAL 3	Turkey Balls	Beef Broccoli	Bred Sticks	Herb Crusted Breast	Turkey Balls	Pepper Lamb Shank	Herb Crusted Breast

121,122	MONDAY	TUESDAY	WEDNESDAY	THURSDAY	FRIDAY	SATURDAY	SUNDAY
MEAL 1	Honey Lamb Chops	Steak Bites	Lamb Leg Roast	Honey Lamb Chops	Beef Carrot Stew	Sausage Balls	Crispy Turkey Strips
MEAL 2	Minced Beef Rice	Citrus Turkey Roast	Steak with Cauliflower	Almond Cake	Chicken Hot Wings	Pork Stew with Veggies	Rosemary Lamb Chops
MEAL 3	Pork Broccoli Stir Fry	Garlic Bread Pizza	Pork Broccoli Stir Fry	Pepper Lamb Shank	Garlic Bread Pizza	Pork Fried Rice	Pork Fried Rice

123,124	MONDAY	TUESDAY	WEDNESDAY	THURSDAY	FRIDAY	SATURDAY	SUNDAY
MEAL 1	Chicken Chimichangas	Fried Turkey Burgers	Beef Carrot Stew	Stuffed Chicken	Lamb Leg Roast	Lamb Skewers	Bell Pepper Lamb
MEAL 2	Chicken Marsala	Coated Apple Chips	Tasty Chicken Wings	Coated Apple Chips	Carrot Cake	Tasty Chicken Wings	Ribeye Fried Steak
MEAL 3	Beef Meatballs	Bell Pepper Lamb	Whole Chicken Roast	Chocolate Muffin	Bell Pepper Lamb	Chicken Indian Kebab	Asian Lamb Chops

125,126	MONDAY	TUESDAY	WEDNESDAY	THURSDAY	FRIDAY	SATURDAY	SUNDAY
MEAL 1	Shredded Chicken	Crispy Pot Roast	Chicken Chimichangas	Steak Bites	Fried Turkey Burgers	Crispy Turkey Strips	Sausage Balls
MEAL 2	Turkey Salad	Pork Stew with Veggies	Chicken Marsala	Pork Chops	Steak with Cauliflower	Pork Chops	Coconut Curry
MEAL 3	Turkey Balls	Crispy Chuck Roast	Beef Curry	Chicken Marsala	Pepper Lamb Shank	Egg Flan	Chocolate Muffin

127,128	MONDAY	TUESDAY	WEDNESDAY	THURSDAY	FRIDAY	SATURDAY	SUNDAY
MEAL 1	Crispy Pot Roast	Spinach Turkey Breasts	Potato Chicken Curry	Lamb Skewers	Shredded Chicken	Shredded Chicken	Chickpea Lamb Stew
MEAL 2	Pork Stew with Veggies	Chicken Marsala	Almond Cake	Pork Stew with Veggies	Brownie	Minced Beef Rice	Coated Apple Chips
MEAL 3	Green Beans Pork Bites	Pork Fried Rice	Bred Sticks	Turkey Balls	Turkey Casserole	Pepper Lamb Shank	Turkey Balls

129,130	MONDAY	TUESDAY	WEDNESDAY	THURSDAY	FRIDAY	SATURDAY	SUNDAY
MEAL 1	Spinach Turkey Breasts	Stuffed Chicken	Fried chicken	Lamb Leg Roast	Sausage Balls	Sausage Balls	Stuffed Chicken
MEAL 2	Steak with Cauliflower	Minced Beef Rice	Coconut Curry	Chicken Marsala	Ribeye Fried Steak	Carrot Cake	Coconut Curry
MEAL 3	Beef Broccoli	Asian Lamb Chops	Garlic Bread Pizza	Pepper Lamb Shank	Crispy Chuck Roast	Turkey Balls	Whole Chicken Roast

131,132	MONDAY	TUESDAY	WEDNESDAY	THURSDAY	FRIDAY	SATURDAY	SUNDAY
MEAL 1	Beef Carrot Stew	Pesto Veggie Pasta	Lamb Skewers	Lamb Leg Roast	Honey Lamb Chops	Chicken Chimichangas	Chickpea Lamb Stew
MEAL 2	Rosemary Lamb Chops	Pork Chops	Chicken Marsala	Carrot Cake	Ribeye Fried Steak	Chicken Hot Wings	Chicken Marsala
MEAL 3	Beef Curry	Pork Fried Rice	Crispy Chuck Roast	Crispy Chuck Roast	Crispy Chuck Roast	Chicken Marsala	Green Beans Pork Bites

133,134	MONDAY	TUESDAY	WEDNESDAY	THURSDAY	FRIDAY	SATURDAY	SUNDAY
MEAL 1	Spinach Turkey Breasts	Crispy Turkey Strips	Crispy Pot Roast	Shredded Chicken	Chicken Chimichangas	Beef Carrot Stew	Steak Bites
MEAL 2	Minced Beef Rice	Chicken Marsala	Tasty Chicken Wings	Rice Pudding	Turkey Salad	Turkey Skewers	Minced Beef Rice
MEAL 3	Beef Meatballs	Egg Flan	Beef Meatballs	Beef Broccoli	Garlic Bread Pizza	Pepper Lamb Shank	Asian Lamb Chops

135,136	MONDAY	TUESDAY	WEDNESDAY	THURSDAY	FRIDAY	SATURDAY	SUNDAY
MEAL 1	Pesto Veggie Pasta	Steak Bites	Potato Chicken Curry	Lamb Skewers	Honey Lamb Chops	Spinach Turkey Breasts	Honey Lamb Chops
MEAL 2	Citrus Turkey Roast	Tasty Chicken Wings	Turkey Stew	Ribeye Fried Steak	Pork Stew with Veggies	Rosemary Lamb Chops	Minced Beef Rice
MEAL 3	Chocolate Muffin	Beef Curry	Beef Meatballs	Chicken Marsala	Herb Crusted Breast	Turkey Casserole	Turkey Balls

Made in the USA
Coppell, TX
20 November 2020